As a leader, you have the power to influence, and you make a choice to either influence negatively or positively.

– Jeffrey Gitomer

Jeffrey Gitomer's

LITTLE BOOK *of* LEADERSHIP

+≡ The 12.5 Strengths ≡+
*of responsible, reliable, remarkable
leaders that create results,
rewards, and resilience*

WILEY

Jeffrey Gitomer's Little Book of Leadership

Copyright © 2011 by Jeffrey Gitomer. All rights reserved.

Published by John Wiley & Sons, Inc., Hoboken, New Jersey
Published simultaneously in Canada

The Little Book Series is a registered trademark of Jeffrey Gitomer.

To order additional copies of this book, contact your local bookseller or call Jeffrey's friendly office at 704/333-1112.

The author may be contacted at the following address:
BuyGitomer
310 Arlington Ave., Loft 329
Charlotte, NC 28203
Phone: 704/333-1112 Fax: 704/333-1011
E-mail: salesman@gitomer.com
Web sites: www.gitomer.com, www.trainone.com

Creative Director: Jessica McDougall
Pagesetting: Michael Wolff
Proofreading: Brad Baker and Claudia Cano
Cover design: Josh Gitomer

Printed in China by RR Donnelley.

ISBN: 978-0-470-94457-8

First Printing, April 2011

Library of Congress Cataloging-in-Publication Data available upon request.

The Time for a Real-World Leadership Book is NOW!

This *Little Book of Leadership* creates a new opportunity for leaders and wannabe leaders who are seeking to achieve, win, and succeed regardless of their title, their status, their place of employment, or their experience.

This is a leadership book that transcends theory and philosophy, and gets right down to brass tacks and brass tactics, and adds a few brass balls.

Everyone knows that leadership takes guts and courage. What many don't understand is that leadership takes a person who can maintain calm and resilience in the middle of the business and government battlefield.

A leader must be able to react to, respond to, and recover from the existing circumstances, often in an instant.

HERE'S HOW YOU CAN WIN: This book will challenge you to self-assess every facet of your leadership ability, and will ask you to evaluate every fact that's given in order to fully understand what actions you need to take and what improvements need to be made in your skills.

How to Use This Book to Succeed...

All leaders want to succeed. This book will help. Its contents are neither a formula nor a manifesto. Rather, they are a collection of principles, ideas, examples, and thought-provoking concepts that will help you succeed as a leader at this moment, in these times.

TAKE ACTION: Look for the key points of understanding and key actions you can take to implement the information.

This book will present things you may never have thought about as a leader: how your attitude affects other's attitudes, how your experience involuntarily kicks in to help you decide in a crisis, and how your resilience helps you accept anything and respond in a way that not only achieves, but also creates opportunity for more achievement.

This book will ask you to think about and re-think the way you delegate and the way you communicate, and to take a closer look at how you are viewed, not just how you view others.

This book will create options for you to see things in a new and different light. It will help you create fresh responses to aide in your collaboration with others – not just to complete a task; but also to earn respect, and consequently your reputation.

This book will help you understand your situation, identify your opportunities, create the your objectives, execute by action and delegation, and establish a leadership position through enthusiasm, brilliance, action, collaboration, resilience, and achievement – not by force, command, title, or entitlement.

LET THIS BOOK BE YOUR MEASURING STICK: This is NOT a book for you to read and say, "I know that." This book will challenge you to ask yourself, "How good am I at that?" and create answers and strategies to close the gap between, "Where am I now?" and "Where do I want to be?"

I'm not questioning your knowledge of things, but this book will create an opportunity for you to turn that knowledge into success and fulfillment.

This book is written about you and for you. My intention was to make it as convenient and actionable as possible:

1. **I made the book little so you can carry it with you.**

2. **I made each chapter short and sweet so you can read it and absorb it in minutes.**

2.5 **And I made this book challenging because as a leader you're seeking challenge.**

This book will take your gray matter to the very end of its synapses.

Define Leadership.
Now Redefine It
In Terms of You.

It occurred to me that most people who write about leadership are no longer leaders. It's easy for those authors to espouse their Monday-morning philosophy – but it's hard for the leaders under fire to take "non-leader" direction.

I just read an article in a business magazine written by a well-known author who used to be a leader. I was horrified. One of the "key" points was that "Clarity is the antidote of anxiety, therefore clarity is the preoccupation of the effective leader." What a bunch of baloney!

If you're a leader, and clarity is your preoccupation, nothing much is going on.

To me, the preoccupation of a leader is multifaceted. There is no "one" preoccupation more powerful than the other. Leading by example, loyalty of team, achievement of goals, profit to company, excellence of performance, great communication skills, and fulfillment on the job are all more important than "clarity." And if a leader isn't a bit "muddy" along the way, something's wrong.

"Clarity is the antidote of anxiety." Bogus. If a leader has anxiety, the first step would be to discover the root of it, and then take action to eliminate it.

Being "clear" is a silly buzzword that means nothing. It's as meaningless as "added-value" or "on-purpose" or "focus." Empty words created about leadership.

So, if you're a boss, manager, or leader of some kind, listen up! I'm going to help you gain understanding about the skills you need to be a true leader. Better stated, what leadership qualities you have to implement to succeed – the action items, principles, and skills to employ so that leadership works. Works for you, your people, your customers, your vendors, and your company. In that order.

Keep in mind that there are degrees of leadership effectiveness. Your ability to master *these leadership skills is in direct proportion to your ability to lead:*

- **Get your people to like you and believe in you.** Hated leaders are eventually overthrown, or fired. Unless you are the ultimate leader, in which case people just quit.

- **Make sure your people and their jobs are a "fit."** People need to feel comfortable about the tasks they are performing every day and the space they're performing them in.

- **Let your people tell you their goals, then modify them together.** If they make them, they believe they can achieve them.

- **Give your people specific tasks and clear direction.** Make sure they know what they're doing and how to do it. And make sure they see the big picture and how their part is vital to it.

- **Get your people to love their work and their workplace.** Make the tasks accomplishable and the workplace fun. Provide a GREAT and happy atmosphere to work in. Make the atmosphere conducive to achievement, and the duty, task, or project challenging without being oppressive or stressful.

- **Make sure that all matters of money are clear.** Don't mess with people's money. And worse, don't reduce pay or commissions to cut costs. Pay fair, benefit well, and provide security. Otherwise people will leave.

- **Make sure their paychecks are accurate and that they clear.** People count their money, and are counting on it. Nothing dings morale more than messed up wages.

- **Encourage your people.** There's nothing better than a coach cheering on his players from the sidelines. Buy every member of your team a copy of *The Little Engine That Could*.

- **Reward your people.** Doesn't always have to be money – although if you ask them what they want, money will always be their answer. Whatever you give them, don't be cheap about it. Make them feel valued.

- **Praise your people.** Praise hard work. Praise effort. Praise accomplishment. Often.

- **Through your actions and achievements, be their hero.** Your people need to see your dedication in order to become dedicated. If you are the one driving the train and making big things happen, you will become the hero of those who respect your ethics and accomplishments.

How's that for a dose of "clarity?"

> There are those who espouse the leadership philosophy of "You don't have to be liked. You just have to be respected." And that is a great statement if you're looking for high turnover.

People will seek to work for people they like AND respect. Let go of your ounce of power. Benevolence works better.

I'm sure you've heard the phrase, "Lead, follow, or get out of the way."

HERE'S A MAJOR CLUE: If you're the leader and you haven't mastered the leadership skills I just listed, you don't have to worry about getting out of the way. Your best people will run you over – or run away from you.

New Thinking About 40 Years of Excellence.

- A note from Paul "Doc" Hersey

More than 40 years ago, I created the criteria, lectures, and books for what would ultimately evolve into Situational Leadership®. Since that time, more than 10 million leaders have been exposed to the classes and the incredible opportunity that this program offers.

Paul "Doc" Hersey

My trademarked and globally recognized "four quadrants and bell curve" has been my personal hallmark of training for every class or seminar I deliver.

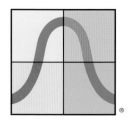

People love it and relate to it. And I'll admit, I'm proud every time I draw it.

While my globetrotting has slowed down as I begin my ninth decade, and many of my day-to-day leadership duties at The Center for Leadership

Studies have been passed to the very strong team I have developed, I am still the "cerebral head," not the "figure head," in planning the next decade of Situational Leadership.

After more than five decades of teaching and thinking, I have come to an additional conclusion about the fundamental execution of Situational Leadership: It STARTS with the attitude (receptiveness) of both the leader and the team members.

Which brings me to the introduction of the attitude genius of my colleague and buddy, Jeffrey Gitomer.

For the past 10 years, our friendship has blossomed because of a mutual exchange of philosophies and ideas, and because his sports memorabilia collection includes ephemera of my basketball teammates at Seton Hall.

Jeffrey's *Little Book of Leadership* is a BIG book.

Besides introducing the revolutionary new look at Situational Leadership for the next 10 years, Jeffrey has examined and refined the characteristics, principles, and strengths of a leader so that they are able to excel at working with and through others in a positive and impactful way.

Contents

1. LEADERSHIP INSIGHT

2. MENTAL LEADERSHIP

3. RESILIENT LEADERSHIP

4. REALITY LEADERSHIP

5. COACH LEADERSHIP

6. (The New) SITUATIONAL LEADERSHIP

7. MEASUREMENT LEADERSHIP

8. OPPORTUNITY LEADERSHIP

9. GUTS LEADERSHIP

STRENGTH

1

LEADERSHIP INSIGHT

The strength, curiosity, and fortitude to understand leadership FIRST, and execute the core principles second.

The 19.5 Principles of Leadership.

Principles guide your life. Principles are character builders. Principles are standards that will lead you to achievement and success. And principles, when applied consistently over time, will build both reputation and legacy.

Here are the 19.5 Principles of Leadership that will enhance your leadership skills and ability to legacy level:

1. Your philosophy of life and leadership determines the process by which you lead. Your philosophy is something you'd want people to talk about at your funeral. It's what you hope will live on within others that you have inspired. *What is your leadership philosophy? What is your life philosophy? Do you understand that your philosophy triggers attitude and guides your actions and your legacy?*

2. Your positive attitude affects everyone around you. Your attitude determines much more than your expressions; your attitude determines your mood, your effectiveness, your thinking, your communications, your actions, and your fate. *How positive is your attitude?*

3. Your experience and past history of success provides comfort and assurance as you make decisions to move forward. Experience makes decision making faster and less complex, and gives you assurance. *Are you using your past successful outcomes to ensure present and future successful outcomes?*

4. When you lead by example, there is nothing your people will not do for you and with you. Don't tell me what to do, show me how it's done. Then delegate. *What kind of example do you set on a daily basis?*

5. Your "likeability" can affect the quality and effectiveness of your leadership. Be or become likeable. If the people on your team like you, and they believe you, and they have confidence in you, and they trust you – then they will follow you. It STARTS with likeability. *How likeable are you?*

6. Clear communication leads to understanding and action. Employees listen very closely to their leaders. But many leaders are not concise in their messaging, and not compelling in their presentation skills. Leaders have a responsibility to their people to deliver actionable messages. Understanding leads to task and project completion. *How certain are you that your communications are compelling and clear?*

7. Responsibility is not given; it's taken. You are responsible for yourself and accountable to and for others. IMPORTANT: The opposite of responsibility is blame. Take responsibility for your actions, your delegations, and especially your words. *How do you take responsibility?*

8. Collaboration will earn respect, results, and reputation. Working WITH your people will create an atmosphere conducive to positive accomplishment. It will also expand thinking and enhance ideas. *Is collaboration a daily part of your leadership responsibility?*

9. Do what you say. Fulfill what you promise. Promises are empty words without action. It's important to keep in mind that you are measured by your words AND your deeds. Your people are measuring you by follow through and by accomplishment. *How do you measure up?*

10. Take more than a minute to praise, coach, inform, and train. There is no such thing as a one-minute manager. How you lead should not be measured in time. Rather, it should be open-ended, quality time. Invest time in your people and their skills; the reward will be years of success and fulfillment. *Is your time spent or invested?*

11. Know the high ground of winning, and the stomping ground of defeat. Leading is not just about winning and losing, it's about the experience gained to move forward. Celebrate the win, strengthen resolve from the loss – learn from both, and move on. *Are you a winner or a whiner?*

12. Resilience is your internal force to react, respond, and recover from events and people. It is the least recognized and least understood facet of the complete leader. Also, arguably the most important element for long-term success. *Do you understand what makes you resilient?*

13. The courage to risk, be right, and be wrong. Risk tolerance is higher in leaders because they know risk is part of winning. You've heard the expression, "No risk, no reward." My statement is, "No risk, no nothing!" People and teams that "play it safe" when they have the lead, usually lose to those who are willing to take risks. *What is your risk tolerance?*

14. Separate task from person. Then assign them and combine them to achieve a positive outcome. A leader is more than a "people person." He or she must also be a task-oriented person. The successful completion of a task is based on the readiness and willingness of the person. The measurement of task success is as important as measurement of human success. *Do you understand the situation? And do you recognize it as situational?*

15. Reward individual and group achievement. Celebrate their victory. Praise their actions, and help them develop a deep sense of pride. CAUTION: Bask in present victory for a moment, but don't dwell on it, or live in it. *How would your people rate your ability to praise and reward them?*

16. You must earn, not command, both trust and respect. "Earn" is THE key word to unlock leadership success. And respect and trust are at the top of a long list of characteristics vital to every leader's core values. You don't just build a reputation; you earn one. Same with loyalty and friendship. It's equally important to know that these attributes are not earned in a day – they're earned, by your words, actions, and deeds, day by day. *Do you earn it or expect it?*

17. Encourage THEIR success to earn and achieve yours. If there is a "lost secret" of leadership it is the word: encouragement. Beyond giving orders, assigning tasks, setting deadlines, and any other aspect of achievement, one "attaboy" or "way to go" or "You can do it!" delivered with genuine emotion, will go a longer way than any command. *How much encouragement do you deliver to your people on a daily basis?*

18. Your ability to influence people will manifest itself in successful outcomes. Influence comes from a base of respected authority and your ability to transfer a message, concept, idea, strategy, or task in a compelling and believable manner. *Are you measuring influence against outcome?*

19. Your reputation precedes you, and defines you. Reputation affects your ability to lead as much as any other arrow in your quiver. Build yours by always "doing the right thing" and adhering to an ethical standard beyond reproach. *How would your people rate your ethics?*

19.5 Legacy is built with single achievements piled high on one another. It's an end result of a lifetime of success. Build yours and the outcome will be lifetime lessons for those that follow you, and an eternal blessing to the ones you love. *Are you aware that you will leave a legacy? What daily actions are you taking toward that legacy?*

WHEW! That's a list of principles and standards fit for a phenomenal human being! And that human can be you.

Start today by reading, studying, and applying the lessons and examples on the pages that follow...

The Respect Factor – Earning Versus Demanding.

Most people expect that with title, respect will follow. And unfortunately most people are wrong.

Your team members don't respect a title until they respect a person. Or I should say it's the characteristics of that person, the actions of that person, and the words of that person that would cause the respect to happen. Or not.

As a leader you have "character." Character that's developed over time from your experiences, your knowledge, and your image. The French term is "Noblesse Oblige" – described as the way you carry yourself; your self-portrait.

When you gain respect, when you *earn* respect, your directions, your delegations, your goals, and your strategies become infinitely more transferable and implementable.

Respect has several levels. You can respect someone face-to-face, in a professional or business environment (that's referred to as formal respect). The most powerful level is absent respect (or genuine respect). It's what other people say about you when you're not there – how they talk about you and how they refer to you. As leader, if you only have professional respect, you will not get the same performance or the same level of dedication from your people as you would if you had genuine respect.

Listen to the tone and look at the facial expressions of the people you interact with every day. If there are no smiles, and if you perceive that full effort is not being given, then all you have is formal respect.

The key to earning respect is not just words, deeds, and actions; it's also consistent words, consistent deeds, and consistent actions that are integrity based, truth based, and ethically based.

Your people will always respect the office, and the title.

HERE'S THE CHALLENGE: Do they respect the person that wears it – or should I say the person who earns it?

KEY POINT OF UNDERSTANDING: If you think respect automatically comes with the title, rethink it.

KEY ACTION TO TAKE: Study your words and actions. Do they deserve respect? Study your reputation. Does it deserve respect?

Do They Want to Listen to You? Or Do They Have to Listen to You?

All leaders have meetings. And their people come to the meeting with an expectation that they will leave better off than when they came. More informed, more directed, more motivated, and more inspired.

NOTE WELL: The conciseness and the clarity of your message is at the very core of meeting your audience's hopes and desires. It will also determine the mood that they're all in when they leave, and what actions they're likely to take upon returning to their office or their destination.

I ask managers and leaders a simple question: Do your people *want* to listen to you, or do they *have* to listen to you? That's not just a tough question; it's also a tough reality. How would your people answer it?

In order to provide effective, actionable, memorable communication – communications that your people want to listen to – you the leader must put preparation and passion into your message. And that message must reek of clarity, understandability, and transferability.

In my speeches, seminars, and workshops I create what are known as *transferable concepts*. A transferable concept should be your goal in every meeting you conduct, in every e-mail you send, in every paragraph you write, and in every "by example" action that you take.

A transferable concept is defined as follows: each member of your team thinks or says to themselves as you're delivering your message and presenting new ideas: "I get it. I agree with it. I think I can do it. I'm willing to try it."

A transferable concept has to be within every idea you put forward, every goal that's given, every concept you present, and every example that you share.

Most leaders think that their position of authority is sufficient to present messages to their team. They are horribly and dangerously wrong.

Over the past 15 years, I have seen more than 2,000 leaders of businesses make presentations. 95% (and I'm being kind with that percentage) were somewhere between bad and pathetic.

Presentation skills, passion, and a compelling message must be combined with understandable, relevant, actionable information, or it's useless – and worse, a wasted opportunity to lead.

People gather to hear what their leader has to say, and are looking for guidance, instruction, and inspiration.

If every leader said… "Men and women of our team, thank you for your service. This year I'm asking you to concentrate on these THREE things. (Name the things.) If you are able to achieve them to the best of your ability, our company will thrive, and so will you and your families. I'm thanking you in advance for meeting this challenge. Please stay in touch with your leaders and me personally, so that I may stay in touch with you." *…he or she would get a standing ovation for a three-minute speech, and no one would be talking or texting during it.*

Anybody texting while you're talking?

KEY POINT OF UNDERSTANDING: Once you realize that your ideas must be transferable, then at once you will understand how important preparation and clarity are in delivering your messages. Your presentation skills and your passion must exist in every communication that you make. And it is equally as important to make certain that what *you* believe is a transferable idea is also an acceptable one to your audience or your people.

KEY ACTION TO TAKE: Select elements from the last several speeches you gave and select elements from the last several e-mails you wrote and ask yourself – better, challenge yourself – about their transferability. Did your people do what you asked them to do? If you were in the audience or were the recipient of the message, would you be taking action, or would you be grumbling?

Your people are a direct reflection of you. They watch you. They follow you. They measure you. They listen to you.
If you want them to be dedicated to you, you have to be dedicated to them.

– Jeffrey Gitomer

STRENGTH

2

MENTAL LEADERSHIP

The mental strength to execute masterful leadership stems from your core philosophical thinking, and your YES! Attitude.

Developing a Leadership Attitude

When I ask, "How's your attitude?" the typical response that I get involves the "moment." Most leaders will say something like, "Do you mean right now?" or "It depends on what my people are doing," or "Call me tomorrow and I'll let you know."

Those responses are not just irresponsible; they're also dangerous. Your attitude is yours, but those types of responses tell me it's dependent on others.

One of the hidden mysteries of success, certainly of leadership success, is the personal attitude of the leader. And how that attitude is developed determines every aspect of their success, their reputation, and their legacy.

Your success, your reputation, and your legacy.

My first question to you is: Have you ever taken an attitude course? **ANSWER:** Probably not.

My second question to you is: Have you ever read an attitude book? **ANSWER:** Probably not.

My third question to you is: How important is the attitude of your people when you're trying to create productivity and achievement? **ANSWER:** That's probably their most important characteristic.

Well, if it's most important with your people, why isn't it most important to you? More succinctly, do you understand how your attitude affects their attitude?

I'll guarantee you that in the course of your leadership tenure, you've hired people because they had great skills and soon after fired them because they had a lousy attitude.

REALITY: Your people and their achievement are a direct reflection and a direct result of your attitude.

Attitude is at the fulcrum point of willingness, of cooperation, of taking action, of achievement, and (of course) of celebrating victory.

I train a lot of big companies, and in every instance I insist that YES! Attitude (positive attitude) training be at the core of any program or initiative or imperative that I launch. Attitude FIRST.

A YES! Attitude is an integral part of your thought process – and your attitude is created by your thoughts.

When something great happens to you, you don't scream, "POSITIVE!" When something great happens to you, you scream, "YES!" The difference is subtle, but completely understandable.

If great attitudes are what you want from your people, then that is where you must start your personal process of great leadership.

Free Git≮Bit... If you would like the formula for what creates a YES! Attitude, go to www.gitomer.com and enter the words ATTITUDE FORMULA in the GitBit box.

KEY POINT OF UNDERSTANDING: Most companies have NEVER given or offered a positive attitude or YES! Attitude course to their employees, yet when I ask prospective customers what the single biggest employee success element is, they ALL respond with "their attitude." Understand that if you don't provide training for attitude, your people will never achieve the level of morale you're hoping for.

KEY ACTION TO TAKE: Before you institute or implement the next "program" at your company, implement the "imperative" of attitude.

Why is YES! Attitude at the Fulcrum Point of Leadership, Managerial, and Workplace Success?

- **Leaders have to be consistent in their performance.** YES! Attitude is the foundation for consistent performance.

- **Leaders must create harmony in the workplace.** YES! Attitude is the foundation for workplace harmony.

- **Leaders want morale to be consistently high.** YES! Attitude is the foundation for high morale.

- **Leaders must create a productive workspace.** YES! Attitude is the foundation for productivity, both individual and team.

- **Leaders and co-workers must communicate inside and outside the workspace.** YES! Attitude is the foundation for positive communication.

- **Leaders and co-workers must respond to others inside and outside the workspace.** YES! Attitude is the foundation for positive response.

YES! Attitude changes minds and lives – at work and at home.

Your YES! inspires their YES!

– Jeffrey Gitomer

Attitude In. Attitude Out. (That's the Real 360.)

Attitude is at the core of success – yours first! If you're a leader that's looking to succeed and leave a legacy of achievement and accolade, then you may want to start higher than your goals and aspirations to uncover the way to make those aspirations a reality.

When you wake up in the morning, how do you feel?

When you get to your place of work, how do you feel?

When you greet members of your team, what is your tone?

When you conduct a meeting, what is your tone?

Here are the attitude questions to ask yourself:

- **How are my people affected by my feelings and tones?**

- **How do my feelings and expressions affect my team's attitude?**

- **How does my attitude impact their responses to me, to each other, and to outside people?**

- **And finally, how does my attitude, my mood, and my tone affect their performance?**

The answer to all of those is TOTALLY!

If your mood is sour, and your words are harsh, what could you possibly expect from the people you work with?

If you've ever started a meeting with the expression, "Okay everybody, I want to see some better attitudes around here!" maybe you should look at the problem rather than the symptom. The remedy to the problem is a simple one. Start with your own attitude.

Whatever you give, you will get.

Starting your day with a YES! Attitude, and communicating those feelings to others is not an option; it's an opportunity. I hope you're taking advantage of your legacy opportunity.

KEY POINT OF UNDERSTANDING: You set the tone for your people to follow. If they're not happy, first look at yourself.

KEY ACTION TO TAKE: Read my *Little Gold Book of YES! Attitude*. TWICE. (This is NOT a commercial; it's my best recommendation for you to expose your attitude to yourself, which is a critical part of the 360 criteria. My book breaks down how to understand attitude, how to make a game plan for self-improvement, and how to achieve a YES! Attitude and keep it for a lifetime.)

It's Not Morale; It's Attitude.

Think about it. If every person on your team had a great attitude, there would never be a morale issue.

The key causes of morale deterioration are:

- **Poor business conditions**
- **Poor work environment conditions**
- **The inability of people to get along with each other**
- **Belligerent leadership**
- **Poor communication**
- **False communication**
- **Financial setbacks**
- **Employee termination**

Many leaders look at it backwards. They say, "We have a morale problem."

Morale is not a problem. Morale is a symptom.

The circumstances that have caused low morale (combined with the attitude of each individual on your team) are what need to be addressed.

CHALLENGE QUESTION: Has everyone on your team taken an attitude course or been formally trained in positive or YES! Attitude?

ANSWER: I doubt it.

BIGGER CHALLENGE QUESTION: (Which I've asked you before.) Have YOU ever taken a course in attitude?

ANSWER: I doubt it.

Take one, and give one, to everyone, as fast as you can.

KEY POINT OF UNDERSTANDING: Once you realize that low morale is a symptom, you can immediately begin to assess the problem or the problems. But simply fixing the problem may not make the morale issue disappear. There must be concurrent attitude training so that as the problem dissipates, the attitudes of your people will simultaneously rise and become more positive.

Free Git Bit... Want to teach your people how attitude is related to success? You can get the simple guide by going to www.gitomer.com and entering the words ATTITUDE GUIDE in the GitBit box.

KEY ACTION TO TAKE: Go back and assess the last time morale was an issue. Review what caused it, what resolved it, and how long it took to get everyone back to full productivity. Think about how much quicker that resolve could have been with the injection of an attitude course to every member of your team, including you.

Developing a Leadership Philosophy.

When I say the words "personal philosophy," what do you think about? When I say the words "leadership philosophy," what words or thoughts come to mind?

Do you understand that philosophies will drive your attitude and your actions? Do you understand if you have no philosophy that you may not have a full understanding of the big picture of your life? Your career? Your beliefs? Your purpose? Your ideals?

SOUND FAMILIAR? You get up in the morning and you drive to work, and you start working, but you don't know why.

HERE'S THE SECRET: "Why" *is* your philosophy!

My objective is to help you uncover your "philosophical why" because everybody has a different one.

If you think your why is money, think again. It's not the money, it's what you will do with the money, or who you will help with the money. That's philosophy. Money is actually a guidepost that will help you understand that where you invest it may be part of your philosophy.

The other part is how you will earn it.

A personal philosophy is not something you have to take a college course in to understand or develop. It contains important things like "be the best dad" or "be the best mom" or "lead with benevolence" or "stay a student" or "become a better community member."

Philosophy is all about the things you want to achieve in your life, and how you intend to achieve them.

Philosophy is NOT about the things you need to achieve in this pay period.

Philosophy is about being the best at what you do, because when you become best, money just follows. When your focus is on the dollar, then you divert attention away from your potential growth, you divert attention away from your personal ability to improve, and you divert attention away from the things that mean the most to you, your spouse, your kids, your parents, and the people that you care about, not the things that you care about.

Once you learn how to understand, identify, build, and develop your personal philosophy, it will be the reward of a lifetime – for a lifetime.

Keep in mind if you're 30, 40, 50, or 60 years old, and you don't have a philosophy that you understand or have articulated yet, then I can't help you develop one in 30 minutes, and neither can you. Philosophy develops slowly, over time, bit by bit, phrase by phrase, dedication by dedication, insight by insight. You develop it as you mature, and you refine it the same way – as you mature.

You may need to do this exercise several times in order to write your philosophy. But I promise you when you do, your personal results will not only be staggering, they will be life changing. They'll bring you understanding and awareness of where you were, where you are, and where you can strive to be. It's not just an action; it's also a deep-rooted thought process, and a deep-rooted belief process that leads to an action – an action that fulfills your purpose.

Your job in this exercise is to think, understand, write, and then begin to live the philosophy that you have written.

NOTE WELL: Most people have not identified their philosophy. Oh, there may be a phrase or two handed down over generations, but nothing structured, nothing concrete, and certainly nothing committed to memory.

You establish and revise the basic principles of your philosophy by exposure to information, your experiences, and listening to the beliefs of others – especially those you respect. You try to only accept "the good stuff" and then adapt it to enhance or change your way of thinking and living.

While you might believe that you determine your own philosophy, much of it is predetermined or influenced by your childhood home environment.

After that, it's up to you to seek influencers and mentors who will affect the way you think and create the motivation that drives your actions.

My philosophy came from a combination of home environment, books, education, mentors, personal development programs, life experience, and observations.

One of my most respected influencers was the late, great Jim Rohn. He was (and still is) considered by many to be America's foremost business philosopher. Recognized as one of the greatest speakers and influencers of all time, Jim developed principles and philosophies growing up on a farm in Idaho, gleaning information and ideals from his dad, and his first employer/mentor.

Some people are under the misconception that their philosophy and their ability to serve are not connected. Wrong. Your philosophy is the umbilical cord that provides the "essence of life" to your ability to serve.

Here is the essence of Rohn's life cycle of success:

> "Philosophy drives attitude.
> Attitude drives actions.
> Actions drive results.
> Results drive lifestyles."

Here is how Rohn broke it down:
- If you don't like your lifestyle, look at your results.
- If you don't like your results, look at your actions.
- If you don't like your actions, look at your attitude.
- If you don't like your attitude, look at your philosophy.

If you think you don't have a personal philosophy, think again! You have one. Like an old book, it may be hidden in the attic of your psyche, dusty and untouched. But it's there inside of you… somewhere.

Discovering your own personal philosophy will help build your self-belief.

Think about what you value in your life, and in your career. Think about and examine the foundation that you have built your life on.

What's important to you? Do you know? You owe the answer to yourself, and to your family.

You can trace your personal philosophy to everything you do. How you act. How you react. How you serve. How you think.

Discovering and defining your own leadership philosophy will help build your character, resilience, resolve, and self-confidence to lead, influence, and inspire others.

Here are some all-across-the-board words to get you thinking both on a personal and leadership level: Help others, lead by example, be loyal to myself and my family, be supportive without being a crutch, solid relationships, value, friendship, quality, humor, health, faith, responsible, educate, learn new things, and have fun.

THINK ABOUT THIS: Learning *new* answers is about exposing yourself to *new* information, and you may be challenging yourself to document your philosophy for the first time.

It starts with a philosophy and attitude of acceptance, no matter what position you're in. It translates into taking loyal actions for yourself first, and others second. The only way to get the philosophical answers you desire is by learning about and revealing you to yourself. So, I challenge you to find your own – your own personal philosophy and your own leadership philosophy. It's time to start writing.

Here's my personal and leadership philosophy: *I give value first. I help other people. I strive to be my best at what I love to do. I establish long-term relationships with everyone. I have fun, and I do that every day. I found out a secret: If you LOVE what you do, all of your days are the same. They are holidays! And I wish the same for you.*

KEY POINT OF UNDERSTANDING: It's not just having a philosophy, it's living your philosophy daily!

KEY ACTION TO TAKE: Write down three things that define and embrace the way you think about your life's goals.

STRENGTH

3

RESILIENT LEADERSHIP

At the fulcrum point of leadership is the essence of your resilient strength. Resilience is your inner strength to take it, your mental strength to react to it, your outer strength to respond to it, and all your strength to recover from it.

THE RESILIENT LEADER: You Are the Essence of Your Reactions, Your Responses, Your Recovery, and Your Reputation.

My Twitter post today read, "Resilience doesn't start with experience – it STARTS with attitude. Your attitude."

It got more than 100 "re-tweets."

Evidently people understood what I was saying and chose to tell others. But since Twitter only allows 140 characters, I wanted to elaborate on the topic of resilience because it has a much deeper meaning than I was able to provide in one tweet.

PICTURE THIS: Your employee says, "I can't finish the project today. It will take me another week."

PICTURE THIS: You have one solid prospective customer left this month and if they don't buy, you don't make your quota. They call you and say, "We've decided to buy from your competition."

PICTURE THIS: Your best employee gives two weeks' notice that he is going to work for the competition.

PICTURE THIS: Your computer crashes and you're not certain when you backed it up last.

PICTURE THIS: You get an e-mail from your boss telling you that they've revised the compensation plan and unless you do 20% more you'll earn 20% less.

PICTURE THIS: You finally get an appointment with the biggest prospect you've ever had. They've agreed to see you for one hour. You arrive and the decision maker doesn't show up.

Those are all real-world occurrences that, as a leader, you have experienced. And it's important to note that all of these challenges test your mental strength.

RESILIENCE is how you react, respond, and recover from those situations, and it starts with your own strength of attitude. If you're easily dismayed, your self-confidence level is low, your self-esteem is lacking, or your self-image is in doubt – each of the "PICTURE THIS" circumstances is taken as a disaster.

Your resilience level (on a 1-100 scale) is under 10. And the ground between 10 and 100 is where your experience combined with your self-education is called into play.

Attitude resilience challenges your thought process to get from a negative response of "woe is me," to more positive responses of "I can deal with this" and "I can overcome this."

It gets you thinking "Here are a few ideas I have right now that will help me" and "Here are the actions I'm willing to take to make things better" and most important "I'm not going to let these events or situations cause me to think ill of myself, or put myself down. Rather, I will use them as motivation to do better."

And keep in mind, that's just the *reaction* part of resilience.

Once you've processed each one of these circumstances and reacted to them mentally, then it's time to respond to them. Your response is a combination of your attitude and your past experience. Your response is your inner strength manifesting itself in words and deeds.

Most people (leaders included) fail to understand that response is triggered by thought. If you use the term "knee-jerk response," it normally means response without thinking, especially in negative situations.

Each one of you has experienced a dumb response. Something like, "I'm doing the best I can" or "I'm just doing what I've been told" or some reply that's *excuse* based rather than *taking responsibility* based.

Anyone can make an excuse.

It takes a person of character to figure out what they can do to respond, be in control of their own emotions, and think quickly on their feet.

It takes a person of character to come up with something that is forward-moving rather than self-defeating, something that's on the offense rather than being offensive, something that states willingness rather than creates a defense, something that says what you can do rather than what you can't, and something that states what could happen rather than restates what just happened.

And keep in mind, that's just the *response* part of resilience.

Now it's time for your resilience to really shine. You've reacted in a positive way, you've responded in a forward-moving way, and now you must *recover* in a personal way – not just with the people involved, but also taking stock of who you are as a person, and learning the lesson of how this will help build you and build your character instead of looking around to see who is to blame, becoming defensive, or making some lame excuse about it or they – never taking responsibility for *you*.

Recovery lays the groundwork for the next reaction.

Recovery after recovery builds the foundation for your resilience. Positive recovery after positive recovery builds a foundation of cement and concrete reinforced with steel rods. Every recovery is one more brick in your foundation of experience.

You build your stature, you build your self-esteem, you build your self-reliance, you build your self-confidence, and you do it all with inner strength combined with mental strength.

You can call it fortitude or you can call it guts, but I'm challenging you to think of it as resilience, because "PICTURE THIS" events are going to happen to you and your people more than once.

Resilience is not what happens to you. It's how you *react* to, *respond* to, and *recover* from what happens to you.

So I've given you the react, respond, and recover elements of resilience. Let me add a .5 to this list of three. *Integrity.*

Every time an opportunity arises, every time your character or your attitude is challenged and you react, respond, and recover in a positive way, you build personal integrity for who you are, and you seek to become.

You never have to talk about it. Others will see it and witness that strength within you. Others will talk about you in a positive way, others will admire you in a verbal and silent way, and others will seek to follow your exemplary way.

KEY POINT OF UNDERSTANDING: Resilience is the true measure of a leader. It's your pluck, your fortitude, your courage, your inner strength, your guts, and your ability to rebound when someone or something knocks you down.

Ask yourself:

- **How do I measure up?**

- **How do I "take it?"**

- **How do I respond when change is imminent or when plans go awry?**

- **How do I respond when asked questions or presented with challenges?**

- **How do I deal with emergencies?**

KEY ACTION I TAKE: (On a personal note) I'll confess that my resilience is challenged daily – not just as a leader, not just as a businessperson, but also as a father, as a grandfather, and as a friend. Resilience knows no boundaries. But every time an opportunity arises to build mine, I eagerly welcome it and all the lessons attached thereto. I hope you do the same.

HERE'S YOUR OPPORTUNITY TO BECOME A RESILIENT (OR A MORE RESILIENT) LEADER: Buy Gitomer and TrainOne have partnered with The Center for Leadership Studies and are now offering a course in *Resilient Leadership*. This dynamic program will test your strengths, expose your vulnerabilities, and reinforce your resilience as a leader and as a person. For more information, call 704/333-1112.

What Can I Do to Beat Stress? What Can I Do to Beat Worry?

These are worrisome and stressful times. War, threats, security, safety, layoffs, cutbacks, slow economy, less business activity, lots of doubt, and lots more uncertainty. Our society is on edge for the first time since WWII, and we are threatened at home for the first time ever.

Many studies have shown that more than half of our country has experienced greater levels of worry and stress since 9/11.

I have been using the theme, "Make sales, not war," to emphasize the fact that you have to change activity and intensity to get over whatever mental blocks stand in the way of achievement. Especially in these times.

I have challenged my readers and my audiences to become sales warriors – to become more intense about getting the sales they deserve even though there may be less sales around.

As a leader, your stress and worry may be intensified because you have to look out for yourself and your team.

That's all the more reason to mitigate your negative, stressful feelings by concentrating on the positive actions that can relieve them.

But in the heat of it all, many people are scared, many people are worried, and many people are stressed out.

Before you can get rid of worry, you must identify its real cause. The real cause of your worry may surprise you.

Here are the **KEY ACTIONS TO TAKE** to beat worry:

Identify. Worry is a symptom, not a problem. Source the cause. Look at the aspects of your life that cause anxiety. What are the other stress points? LIST ALL YOUR CAUSES. If you tried to plug five or six things into one electrical outlet, it's likely you would blow a fuse. It's the same with you. If you identify the causes, you can unplug a few things by taking them out of your daily routine.

Plan. Once you identify the area that causes worry, change the worry item into an action plan for success. Write a separate plan for each item. Create ways to look at it differently, adopt a new (and better) attitude toward it, or just avoid it. Don't be afraid or embarrassed to enlist the aid of others. They may be glad to help you (and help themselves at the same time).

Read. Reading helps you give your mind YOUR CHOICE of input. Reading gives you a mental rest or mental boost. Reading forces you to turn OFF the TV. The BEST book on the subject of stress and worry was written 50 years ago. It is Dale Carnegie's *How to Stop Worrying & Start Living*. Have you read it? Buy it. Read it.

Sweat. Jog. Work out. Shower. Physical exercise followed by relaxation will clear your mind so you can refocus it. Positive ideas and innovative thoughts will just pop in. I promise. Relax. Walk. A two-block walk clears the head and solutions will follow. Watch an old funny movie (WC Fields, Marx Brothers) or a funny TV rerun (*Honeymooners*). Clear your mind with fresh air and fresh humor.

Act. Don't act ON the worry, act AGAINST it by creating a positive reaction to the worry. I've had a statue on my bookshelf since 1959. It's a ceramic bust of *MAD Magazine's* Alfred E. Newman, smiling with one front tooth missing. Inscribed on the statue is his famous (only) quote, "What – Me Worry?" It's been my credo for more years than I care to acknowledge, but it's also one of the deep, dark secrets of success (or cause of failure). There's nothing to worry about. You're not ill; you're just ill-prepared. You've got the total cure within you. WORK HARDER. Concentrate on the action (solution) that will bring you a reward (personal or monetary) and the worry automatically goes away.

Smile. It's contagious. It sets a good mood both externally and internally. If you do it all the time, every day for 30 days, it will become a habit.

HERE'S A SUCCESS TACTIC: After taking action you must still "let the worry go" mentally. The secret is simple. Release it by smiling. Your smile has the power to turn a negative into a positive, and expel it from your system.

It is critical to realize that stress and worry are not someone else's fault. You bring it on yourself.

There is only one sure thing you can get from worry and stress. A heart attack. The alternative is much better and much more fun – you can proactively attack your worries and create a positive environment for all to reap the benefits.

Free Git Bit... If you'd like insight about things that may be adding additional worry without you realizing it, and a few more actions you can take to release worry and stress, go to www.gitomer.com and enter the words WORRY FREE in the GitBit box.

Resilience doesn't start with experience – it STARTS with attitude – your attitude.

So does leadership.

– Jeffrey Gitomer

Resilience is...

RESILIENCE IS INNER STRENGTH.

Your ability to accept what has been done and/or what has been said in a manner that challenges your character and fortitude, but does not shake it. Not simply taking it in, but also processing it in a way that reflects your true leadership ability, and prepares you to react and respond.

RESILIENCE IS PRESENTING SIMPLE AND UNDERSTANDABLE ANSWERS TO COMPLEX PROBLEMS.

Oftentimes, your resilience is challenged by the complexity of an issue or situation. Especially if your response or decision is urgently required. Your responsibility as a resilient leader is to make certain that your responses are both understandable and actionable. If both of those elements are not present, the problem or the situation will be exacerbated rather than resolved.

RESILIENCE IS BEGINNING RESPONSES WITH QUESTIONS RATHER THAN ANSWERS.

When leaders immediately respond with statements, it's often without the full understanding of what the circumstance is. By asking additional questions and creating responses in the form of "what if…" it creates a collaborative resolution rather than a dictatorial one. One major key to resilience is your *positive* vulnerability to accept the answers and ideas of everyone.

RESILIENCE IS ATTITUDE BEFORE LEADERSHIP.

If your mood is not upbeat, if your mood is not positive, then the likelihood of your reactions and responses being positively received, and acted on, are diminished. And it may even mean short-term failure. Attitude is so important to resilience that its absence challenges the very core of the process. You may have strength, you may have the resolve, you may have the confidence, you may have the experience, but those characteristics must be combined with your personal YES! Attitude in order to create real response, real productivity, real morale, and real outcome – also known as *real resilience*.

RESILIENCE IS ABOUT RESPONDING AND RECOVERING IN A WAY THAT LEADS TO A POSITIVE OUTCOME.

Leadership combines process with outcome. Resilient leadership combines positive process with positive outcome.

YOUR RESILIENCE IS SEEN AND MEASURED BY OTHERS.

Resilient leadership manifests itself in the word of mouth of others and your reputation. It's important that you, as a resilient leader, have enough strength of character to receive this word of mouth, this feedback, in a manner that creates new learning and growing opportunities. This is especially true among leaders with more than 10 years of experience. Resilience also means that you're able to accept, learn, and grow as a result of measured impacts and outcomes. To the resilient leader, continued growth is not an option.

STRENGTH

4

REALITY LEADERSHIP

The strength to understand, apply, become proficient at, and finally master the fundamental aspects of leadership, and the reality of what you need to do to make it YOUR reality.

The 9.5 Tragic Flaws of Leaders.

Every leader has flaws. Even you and me. A successful leader can recognize them and keep them at a minimum.

1. Being a bully leader. There's a big difference between pushing people around, barking orders, and earning cooperation. The manner in which you assign tasks and responsibilities will determine the enthusiasm by which your people will produce and achieve. Bullying also creates low morale and sometimes resentment, both spoken and unspoken. You don't have to be pals with everyone, but you do have to get your way without demeaning others. There's a direct correlation between how people are treated and how people produce. Fear is not a motivator. Encouragement is. All bully leaders eventually fail and fall.

2. Being inaccessible. Every leader has a face. And the more your face is present, the more you will be in touch with what's going on, and the more your people will perceive you as accessible. Everyone wants their minute or two to question the leader, report to the leader, and brag about their successes. They also need to be reassured that everything is going good and will be okay. Accessibility also increases productivity because you're there to provide answers and keep everything moving.

3. Responding or deciding slowly. With the advent of e-mail and texting, any one of your people can reach you in an instant. And (not surprisingly) they expect a reply with the same speed. Sometimes the reply is simple, but many times your reply requires a decision or a direction. Too many times I've heard people say, "My boss decides too slowly" or "I can't get a decision." Your leadership requires decisiveness at net speed – so do your productivity and your profitability. Your responsiveness (or lack of it) also sets a tone for their urgency.

4. Reprimanding in public. This rule of leadership is so old I'm almost embarrassed to write about it. But I have to because it's still one of the most violated rules of leadership. If you have to reprimand someone, if you have to yell at someone, or if you have to tell someone what they've done wrong, take them aside to a private area and do so. This allows your people to keep their dignity, tie their bootlaces tighter, and come back for another day. Their loss of dignity is your loss of integrity.

5. Not keeping promises (or breaking them). Your people live and die by your words. Many of them have longer memories than elephants. What may seem like a minor promise to you might be a major promise to them. Your responsibility is to record (in some manner) every promise that you make to every person on your team so that you will become known as a person who keeps their word, and does what he or she says they're going to do.

6. Not telling the truth. Truth breeds trust; lack of it erodes trust. Truth is easily defined: When you tell it, you never have to remember what you said.

7. Playing favorites. I learned about equal treatment in 1972 when my twins, Stacey and Erika, were born. One could never be favored over the other. Sure, you as leader are going to like some people more than others. Sure, you as leader are going to favor some people who are better performers than others. But you cannot do it to a point where it begins to breed resentment or loss of morale. Find ways to reward everyone on your team in some manner and find ways to praise everyone on your team in some manner. I fully recognize the world is not equal. In 1939, George Orwell wrote, "All animals are equal, but some animals are more equal than others." Your job as leader is to make certain that each person feels great about him or herself, and a large part of that stems from your ability to communicate that message to them.

8. Being in an inconsistent mood. If you're striving for consistency and achievement with your people, then your mood – to make that happen – must be a consistent one. If your people have to wonder, "Is he/she in a good mood today?" something is drastically wrong. Your mood sets their tone.

9. Being out of technological touch. Many leaders are not as in touch with today's world as they could be or should be. As a 65-year-old leader, I'm constantly upgrading my skills and my technology in order to be as current as, or more current than, my people. Internet adeptness, social media presence, and texting are no longer an option. But many leaders are ignorant about all three. It's not about being up to date with the news or what's on TV; it's about being up to date and in touch with everything about your company, your industry, your people, and yourself.

9.5 Assigning the wrong task to the wrong person. The old expression is "a round peg in a square hole." It's the easiest way to define making an incorrect delegation or assigning a wrong task. Oftentimes you will assign an important task to your best person, when in fact they may be the wrong person to complete it. They may even be resentful of the fact that you assigned it to them. The key is collaboration. Meet with your best people for an open discussion and throw the topics of who should be assigned what tasks. Not only will you gain their truth, you will also gain their respect for involving them in the decision-making process.

WHAT ARE YOUR FLAWS? Document them in a positive way. Not what they are. Rather, what their remedy is.

Work in harmony with your people. Be accessible. Respond directly. Reprimand in private. Keep promises, Be truthful. Treat everyone equal. Be in a (consistent) positive mood.

KEY POINT OF UNDERSTANDING: The reality leader, the resilient leader, will tackle their flaws in a different way than ordinary leaders. The ordinary leader will read this list and move on. The extraordinary leader (the resilient leader) will seek to turn a flaw into a strength by creating an action plan for greater self-discipline.

KEY ACTION TO TAKE: On a note card, list the remedies of your flaws on a note card. Put the card in your wallet – next to your money – so that every time you're spending dollars you can think about the actions you need to take to invest in yourself.

Why Can't You Achieve the Goals You Set? Why Can't Your People?

Got goals?

Millions of words have been written about goals (I've written thousands of them), and 99% of those words focus on "how-to" set and achieve them in one form or another. Books, articles, videos, seminars, online courses, and classroom learning.

Everyone sets goals. Some people set them on their own, others have them set for them (sales goals, sales plans, sales quotas). Some people make elaborate game plans for goal achievement, others write them down in their day planner, while still others just cut out a picture from a magazine depicting something they wish they had, but don't (car, boat, house, vacation).

Me? I post my achievement and improvement goals on my bathroom mirror. In plain sight.

Many passé seminar leaders and motivational speakers claim that "less than four percent of all people set goals." Baloney. Everyone has a goal, or many goals. If you're looking for a category that fits the four percent number, it's the people that actually *achieve* the goals they set.

Ever set a goal you failed to achieve? Ever stop in the middle of a goal? Ever fall back to your old ways? Ever miss your sales goals? Of course you have. Everyone has. Want to know why?

Enter Ali Edwards. And my personal biggest AHA! about goals. She has the answer.

On Ali's website, www.aliedwards.com, she asks her readers (me among them), "What are your *intentions*?" It was a WOW! an AHA! and a WAY COOL! all at the same time.

Goals and intentions are linked. Intentions actually trump goal setting. If you fall short of intention, you will not likely achieve the goal you set. What a simple, powerful concept. And, what a truth.

Ali simply asks, "What are your intentions? What do you intend to do?" And the rest of the actions to achieve those intentions will follow.

Goals or intentions – which are more powerful?

You may have a goal, or you may have been given a goal, but whatever your intentions are will dictate the outcome of the effort to achieve, or lack of it.

What do you intend to do?
How do you inspire or influence your people to intend?

Think about these questions:

What do you want to do?

What do you need to do?

What do you have to do?

What do you believe you're capable of doing?

What do you love to do?

How much do you love what you do?

Do you dislike what you do?

Now, maybe you can better answer, what do you *intend* to do?

What you intend to do are the thoughts behind your actions. Intentions are the justification behind your words and deeds. If you intend to manipulate, your words and deeds will follow. If your intentions are pure, your words, deeds, and actions will follow. If you intend to achieve your goals, or a specific goal, your words and deeds will follow.

IMPORTANT LEADERSHIP PERSPECTIVE: I believe that love and intentions are connected more passionately than fear and intentions, or greed and intentions. There's an old quote that says, "The road to hell is paved with good intentions." I wonder how true it is? Personally, I believe the opposite.

There are types of intentions. The easiest to define are "good" and "bad." To intend to do the right thing, or intend to do the wrong thing. Sometimes your intention to do the wrong thing is justified by the way you feel. You believe someone "deserves" what you're about to do. I believe that's the "hell" intention.

There's also an intention to do nothing. Stay away from it. It jeopardizes your position and your reputation as a leader who gets things done.

Great leaders intend to do what's best for the situation at hand and what's best for the long-term interest of everyone – your company, yourself, and your people. And that's the BEST intention of all.

KEY POINT OF UNDERSTANDING: Whatever your intentions are, they form the basis for your actions, the foundation for the achievement of your goals, the manifestation of your desires, and ultimately the fulfillment of your dreams. Simply put, what you intend to do is what you actually do. Goals notwithstanding, it's all about your intentions.

KEY ACTION TO TAKE: Write down your intentions BEFORE you write your goals. Start each sentence with, "I intend to..." or even bolder, "By the end of the week I intend to..." Timing your intentions makes them much more real. An easy way to make your intentions clear is to categorize them. Organize the categories – then write the words to define them. Single words for categories, and sentences to define your intentions. Categories like personal, leader, job, career, study, read, business, life, family, money, fun, travel, and passion. You get the idea.

Manage Yourself... Lead Others.

There are two unfortunate, universal misconceptions among every bad manager:

1. They think they're doing a great job.

2. They don't consider themselves leaders.

Many managers have risen through the ranks by superior performance and are made managers/leaders without any (or minimal) training.

Most of these "managers" will fail their company twice. Once, because they are unprepared for the job, and once because they have left their former position of superstar, creating a productivity void.

Here are a few leadership challenges for you to ponder:

- Are you a leader or manager?

- Are leaders born or made?

- Are you tired of being a manager?

- How do you approach leadership?

- What are the leadership skills you need to develop?

Most managers don't understand the difference between managing and leading.

Here are two axioms to embrace:

1. **No one wants to be managed, but everyone wants to be led.**

2. **There are no world-class managers – only world-class leaders.**

If you insist on managing someone, manage yourself!

Want to be a better leader? Here's what it takes:

- **MAINTAIN A POSITIVE ATTITUDE.** Solution oriented. Action oriented. People oriented. Your enthusiasm begets success.

- **EMBRACE CHANGE.** Change is certain. Followers tend to resist change. It is the mark of a leader to embrace change and take advantage of the opportunity it presents.

- **DEPLOY COURAGE.** Douglas MacArthur said, "Courage is just fear that holds out a little longer." Good advice. George Patton said, "I don't take counsel from my fears." Good advice. Leaders choose courage.

- **TAKE A RISK.** The biggest risk is to never take one. Leaders are determined to win or try again.

- **COMMUNICATE.** Leaders set the example for open communication. Use your head. Say what you feel. Speak from your heart.

- **LISTEN.** Leaders listen to learn. Leaders listen to understand. Your team has needs – just listen. Your prospects and customers know their needs, and they know what's happening on the front lines of their business, and yours – just listen.

- **DELEGATE AND EMPOWER.** Leaders share responsibility. They don't dictate, they set examples for others to follow. Leaders encourage growth in others by challenging them to take new responsibility, encouraging them to succeed, and supporting them if they fail. Leaders understand that mistakes are lessons on the way to success.

- **UNDERSTAND OTHERS, YOURSELF, AND YOUR SITUATION.** Leaders understand the importance of an open, inquisitive mind. A constant quest for knowledge brings greater understanding. Understand yourself first.

- **COMMITMENT.** Commitment is the catalyst that makes all the other leadership qualities a reality. Daily re-dedication to commitment is the difference between leaders and would-be leaders.

Leadership is best learned assessing, understanding, and THEN doing. Start small. Lead a group or committee. Do whatever is necessary to make it a winner. Do it again until it begins to feel natural. Respect the power of leadership and the power of the people you seek to lead. Don't try to OVERpower them, just influence and guide them.

Positive leadership on the job will dictate happiness and success.

There is also the mundane, but important, side of leadership – these tasks and attributes are mostly associated with "managers," but must be mastered by great leaders as well.

Here are 6.5 everyday duties you must perfect in order to be an effective leader:

1. Administrating. Setting policy, dealing with reports, making sure the flow of paper (from orders in to commissions out) is error free. Coordinating the selling, delivering, and servicing process. *Tactic: Delegate what you can't do.*

2. Recruiting. Going out to find (and solicit) people who are the best qualified to sell for your company. *Tactic: Be attractive. By establishing and maintaining an energetic, growth-oriented work environment, you make just working for your company a benefit.*

3. Hiring. Determining by questions, responses, and gut feeling who is a great candidate for, and most likely to succeed at that position. When a person is selected, an integral part of the hiring process is to fully explain all expectations of the job; to set and agree upon goals (a nicer word for quotas); and to get and give commitments of specific performance. The best way to do this is to draft a commitment document that has listed what the company will do and what the person will do. Be specific as to goals to be met. Have both parties sign the document. It should be reviewed in every performance evaluation. *Tactic: Hire happy people. Hire eagles.*

4. Training. If you want to win, win, win, you'd better train, train, train. Managers should lead weekly training meetings, do on-the-job training with the staff, attend every seminar possible, listen to management and leadership CDs in the car every day, and read six books a year on management, leadership attitude, and personal development. *Tactic: Don't just give training. Take it.* (REAL-WORLD NOTE: *Poor performance is not the manager's or leader's fault. It's the fault of the company president for not providing adequate training, or not selecting the right person for the job or both.*)

5. Motivating and Inspiring. If you want success, you must create an atmosphere in which success can occur. This means a continuous (every minute) positive attitude atmosphere must exist. It means recognizing and rewarding great performance. Leaders create this atmosphere. What kind of atmosphere, recognition, and attitude comes from you as a manager/leader? If the atmosphere is lacking, or if a manager is using his or her ounce of power to show "who's boss," I guarantee three things will happen: (1) There will be a high turnover of people; (2) The manager will blame everyone else but himself; and (3) The manager will eventually get the deserved "ax" after doing untold dollars in damage. *Tactic: Achieve and maintain a positive attitude 24 hours a day, seven days a week. Encourage others at every opportunity.*

6. Leadership Skills. Managers (and trainers) who don't lead every day lose touch with reality. How can you lead your people if you don't know what the customer's current needs are? There should be a regular pattern of working

WITH your people. The rule is simple: If you aren't leading and learning, you can't be a leader. *Tactic: Be a better person than your people. Be the best person in your company.*

6.5 Leading by example. This applies to all aspects of the six areas above. Don't *tell* someone how to do something – *show* someone how to do something, and provide the support and training to get it done. As a leader you want your team to succeed. The best way to do this is to lead the way. *Tactic: It's up to you to provide the atmosphere, encouragement, tools, and training so that success can occur.*

When you are asked to join a leadership team after an incredibly successful stint as an employee, do it on one condition. Take six months of intensive, hands-on leadership training before you accept the position. How many months (weeks, days – okay, *hours*) of leadership training have you had? The unfortunate answer for most is: *Not enough.*

HERE'S THE SECRET: Stop managing. Start leading. Your people are counting on you.

How You Train Determines Their Results – and Yours.

Every leader will extoll the value, virtues, and importance of training. Lip service.

In my experience, training departments are not only weak, but incestuous; they also are the FIRST to get budget cuts in lean times. There's more, but let me just get to some answers that will help.

REALITY: Your people want to hear your messages and receive your guidance. Directly from you. They want to have your insight and experience transferred to them directly.

REALITY: Training and facilitating is WAY different from just giving a speech. It's slower, requires transferable concepts, and requires major interaction, role playing, and real-world examples. Show me, don't tell me. Training requires repetition and patience.

REALITY: Leaders must understand that each learner has his or her own pace and method of acceptance.

Here are some key insights of how to increase the effectiveness and outcomes of the training process:

- **Recognize that the responsibility for outcome rests on the ability of the trainer to be compelling – and the content to be engaging.**

The combination of these two elements makes a successful connection.

- Earlier I discussed and defined a transferable concept (page 25) – the audience members must say to themselves, "I get it. I agree with it. I think I can do it. I'm willing to try it." The transferable concept leads to educational and career advancement.

- The learner goes through four stages: 1. Understand. 2. Apply/take action. 3. Become proficient through repetition. 4. Build on personal proficiency to master the concept and the process.

- Classroom success is most easily achieved when you dedicate yourself to making training fun and keeping it real (all about today and tomorrow, not yesterday).

- Repetition is the mother of mastery. You must have a plan in place to create repeated messages (short vignettes of applicable information) in the classroom, online, and in other media forms – text, audio, and video.

- 360 feedback from the class, and from the office or the field where the ideas and strategies have been put forth. Measurement of training is not an option.

- It starts with YES! Attitude. If the trainer does not have a YES! Attitude and the class members do not have a YES! Attitude, don't start.

The new world of learning requires much more than rhetoric and programs to be effective. It requires a series of elements that MUST be present, or the training won't produce the results that senior leadership is hoping for.

Here are the uncompromising elements that successful training must include:

- **The world-class, real-world expertise of the trainer – one or many**
- **Acceptability of the trainer to the students**
- **Acceptability of the content to the students**
- **Willingness of the students to learn and apply**
- **Relatable ideas and concepts to each participant**
- **Proven strategies – no theory or pie in the sky**
- **Real-world, personalized information in harmony with the market**
- **Real-world, personalized information in harmony with the day-to-day job**
- **Transferable concepts that learners can see themselves doing**
- **A learning environment that encourages students to succeed**
- **Actionable elements that can be used immediately and successfully**
- **Timed online reinforcement must exist beyond the classroom lessons**

- **Using the voice of the customer to reinforce the lesson's validity**

- **Using the voice of the customer to reinforce the learner's belief**

- **Measurable success by seven simple measurements – increase in productivity, performance, morale, sales, customer loyalty, employee loyalty, and profit. More significant than ROI or some other phony justification measurement**

- **Before, during, and after the training, leadership that coaches with encouragement on a daily basis**

REALITY: In this economy you need real answers. You cannot take a chance on unproven facts or people.

KEY POINT OF UNDERSTANDING: Your people are a direct reflection of you. They watch you. They follow you. They measure you. They listen to you. If you want them to be dedicated to you, you have to be dedicated to them. Train them to be their best and do their best. Help them to be their best. Encourage them to be their best. Lead them to be their best.

KEY ACTION TO TAKE: Identify the REAL-WORLD needs of your people, and create answers based on your customer's opinions and reasons for buying and doing business with you. Then find someone who can deliver a compelling, inspirational message that encourages your team to create the two things that will win in this economy: more business and more profit.

Self-Evaluation of the Basic Elements of Leadership

AM I THE LEADER I WANT TO BE? Leaders rarely get to evaluate themselves. Below is your opportunity to take a brief look in the mirror. Take a few moments and give yourself an honest response as to your present skill level.

NOTE WELL: If you only look at this list and don't actually circle a number, you will not improve, nor will you have a guideline by which to do it. When you circle the numbers, you're telling yourself where you are and giving yourself an opportunity to grow to where you want to be.

This is a self-evaluation of the basic elements of leadership. To determine where you stand, circle the number to the right of each statement that represents your personal status.

(1=never, 2=rarely, 3=sometimes, 4=regularly, 5=all the time)

☐ **I maintain a consistent positive attitude.**　1　2　3　4　5

☐ **I embrace change as opportunity.**　1　2　3　4　5

☐ **I deploy courage.**　1　2　3　4　5

☐ **I take risks.**　1　2　3　4　5

☐ I listen with the intent to understand. 1 2 3 4 5

☐ I communicate to be understood. 1 2 3 4 5

☐ I delegate and empower others. 1 2 3 4 5

☐ I understand others. 1 2 3 4 5

☐ I understand myself. 1 2 3 4 5

☐ I understand my situation. 1 2 3 4 5

☐ I am committed to being my best. 1 2 3 4 5

☐ I administer with excellence. 1 2 3 4 5

☐ I am able to recruit the best people. 1 2 3 4 5

☐ I hire the best people. 1 2 3 4 5

☐ I retain my best people. 1 2 3 4 5

☐ I train everyone and myself. 1 2 3 4 5

☐ I consistently motivate my team. 1 2 3 4 5

☐ I consistently inspire my team. 1 2 3 4 5

☐ I lead by example. 1 2 3 4 5

Total your circled numbers from the previous pages.

Leadership Scorecard

85-95   **You are the leader I want to be taken to.** This book will help you strengthen and reinforce every aspect of your excellence.

75-84   **You're a good leader.** Dedicated and focused. You're now ready to go from proficiency to mastery.

67-74   **You're a leader, slightly out of focus.** The strengths in this book will help you get back to 20/20 vision.

59-66   **You're leading, but you lack high-level skills.** Dedicate yourself to mastering the fundamental concepts in this book.

40-58   **You're struggling to lead.** Read this book twice, taking notes as you go, THEN make personal plans to master the strengths in this book before you assume any more leadership responsibilities.

GO BACK: Check the box to the left of any element where you circled a 1, 2, or 3. Use the checked boxes to create your personal game plan by creating an action plan for how you will master each element you need to improve on.

Free Git✗Bit...For a PDF version of this test to post where you can see it every day, go to www.gitomer.com and enter the words LEADER TEST in the GitBit box.

4

Don't Ask Me, Ask Yourself!
How RARE Are You?

RETENTION

The "cost of lost" appears on no P&L. It appears on no balance sheet. But it must be known by every leader in order to effectively grow profitability.

How does my percentage of turnover rank against the dollars it costs to train their replacements?

ATTRACTION

A key measurement of success is referred employees. Someone who thinks their job is so great that they want to refer their qualified friends.

How many good people are referred by other employees to come work for me?

REPUTATION

Your reputation is determined by others, especially the people you work with.

How do present and former employees talk about me behind my back?

ENVIRONMENT

When morale is high, productivity is higher.

How happy are my people? How good am I at making their workplace happy? (HINT: How happy am I?)

Leaders Can Help or Hurt, It's Up to You!

More business and profit are lost through poor leadership than through poor performance. Managers/leaders/owners can encourage or discourage people with their policies and actions. What's makes a great leader? Often if you ask a leader, and then ask someone who works for him, you will get two completely different answers.

And keep in mind, that's also leadership through the eyes of salespeople and sales leaders. The people most measured in any company.

I've compiled the following list of leadership attributes from three sources: my personal experience, interviewing leaders, and asking their people, "What makes an ideal leader?" How many of the following attributes describe the way you lead? And if you're an employee reading this, how many of these traits do you wish your boss, leader, or manager had?

- **Lead (manage) by example.** Don't preach things you don't follow or do yourself. You're not above it. Lead by doing – not telling.

- **Get and maintain a positive attitude.** The single biggest step you can take toward your success and the success of your people. Keep your team happy by setting a happy example.

- **Set and achieve goals together with your team.** Don't set quotas, set goals. Review their progress weekly.

- **Take customer and vendor calls.** Stay on top by knowing what the customer needs, what the vendor wants, and by sharpening your ability to listen, understand, and respond.

- **Attend meetings and conferences with your staff.** Walk in their shoes on a regular basis.

- **Make some customer follow-ups on the phone.** Keep in touch with customers to find out what it takes to make them loyal.

- **Take some customer complaint calls.** Find out what the problems and challenges of your customer, your company, and your team really are. Make calls to dissatisfied customers to follow up on actions taken.

- **Make calls to lost customers.** Find out why you lost them.

- **Make customer thank you calls after a sale.** A personal call from management makes a great beginning to a relationship.

- **Call loyal customers.** Find out what makes your customers happy and what kind of job your sales and service people are doing.

- **Ask for feedback.** From employees, upper management, and customers.

- **Put feedback into action.** Show the staff you're listening. It will encourage more productive suggestions and boost morale big time. Show you have the ability to change and grow.

- **Visit your key accounts with your salespeople.** Go on at least five customer calls per month. Stay in the loop.

- **Use project progress reports that are by task rather than by day.** Have activities by task or project so you can see the work progress cycle on one sheet. It's a total waste of time to know what someone did on a Monday or Tuesday.

- **Check on all reports periodically.** Make sure your people aren't just filling spaces to make it look good.

- **Back your staff.** When a customer has a problem, defend and believe in the capability of your people. Don't judge until you've heard both sides.

- **Say nice things to your staff on a regular basis.** Have 10 times as many nice things to say as bad things. Encourage success with support.

- **Encourage, don't reprimand.** Everyone makes mistakes, even you. Encouragement and positive reinforcement will prevent many more mistakes from being made than a reprimand will. Be a coach. Offer support.

- **If you must reprimand, do it in private.** And don't tell anyone else about it.

- **Don't play favorites.** It will kill you, morale, and your most favored.

- **Make your office a fun place to go.** Do people say "uh oh" when asked in?

- **Be inspirational.** Send inspirational messages. Look around your office. Are there inspirational things on the wall? Do you follow those messages, or are they just a hollow reminder of what you should be doing too?

- **Offer rewards and give awards for exceptional work.** Incentives work. Offer incentives that anyone can win.

- **Be known as the person who follows through and gets the job done no matter what.** Or else you will die on the job.

- **Keep your eyes open for the opportunity to improve.** When you're sharp, alert, and getting results, it will inspire your staff.

- **Train, Train, Train.** Train weekly, attend every seminar possible, absorb audio, watch video programs daily, and read books having anything to do with leadership, workforce, loyalty, and positive attitude. And don't just give training. Take it, too.

- **High turnover?** If you continue to lose people, you may want to take a closer look in the mirror. It may not be them.

- **Having fun?** Maybe if there were more mirth in the office there would be better productivity and morale, not to mention lower turnover.

- **Don't manage anyone except yourself.** Be a thinker, a teacher, a coach, an influencer, an encourager, a communicator, a student, an action taker, an example setter, and a leader.

To be a great leader of people – inspire them to follow you, not your rules.

– Jeffrey Gitomer

Self-Evaluation of the Attributes of an Ideal Leader.

DO I POSSESS THE ATTRIBUTES OF AN IDEAL LEADER?

Leaders rarely get to evaluate themselves. Below is your opportunity to take a brief look in the mirror. Take a few moments and give yourself an honest response as to your present skill level.

I just gave you the leadership traits list – and you were shaking your head and nodding like mad.

Now here's your opportunity to get from "I know that" to "How good am I at that?"

This is a self-evaluation of the attributes that can make you or break you. To the right of each statement below, circle the number that best defines you.

(1=never, 2=rarely, 3=sometimes, 4=regularly, 5=all the time)

❑ **I lead (manage) by example.**   1   2   3   4   5

❑ **I have and maintain a positive attitude.**   1   2   3   4   5

❑ **I set and achieve goals together
with my team.**   1   2   3   4   5

❑ **I take inquiry calls.**   1   2   3   4   5

☐ **I make calls and attend meetings with my staff.**   1   2   3   4   5

☐ **I make phone call follow-ups to customers.**   1   2   3   4   5

☐ **I take some customer complaint calls.**   1   2   3   4   5

☐ **I make calls to lost customers.**   1   2   3   4   5

☐ **I make customer thank you calls after a sale.**   1   2   3   4   5

☐ **I call or visit loyal customers with my salespeople.**   1   2   3   4   5

☐ **I use reports that give me productive information.**   1   2   3   4   5

☐ **I check on reports periodically.**   1   2   3   4   5

☐ **I ask for feedback.**   1   2   3   4   5

☐ **I put feedback into action.**   1   2   3   4   5

☐ **I back my staff.**   1   2   3   4   5

☐ **I give positive feedback to my staff on a regular basis.**   1   2   3   4   5

☐ **I encourage rather than reprimand.**   1   2   3   4   5

☐ **If I must reprimand, I do it in private.**   1   2   3   4   5

☐ **I don't play favorites.**   1   2   3   4   5

☐ I'm inspirational.   1 2 3 4 5

☐ I offer rewards/give awards
   for exceptional work.   1 2 3 4 5

☐ I make my office a fun place to work.   1 2 3 4 5

☐ I follow through and get the job done.   1 2 3 4 5

☐ I recognize the opportunity to
   improve or serve.   1 2 3 4 5

☐ I train, train, train.   1 2 3 4 5

☐ My turnover is low.   1 2 3 4 5

☐ I have fun!   1 2 3 4 5

☐ I don't manage anyone except myself.   1 2 3 4 5

NOW GO BACK: Check the box to the left of any attribute where you circled a 1, 2, or 3. Use the checked box statements to construct your personal game plan by creating an action plan for how you will master each of the attributes you need to improve on.

IF YOU'RE SERIOUS ABOUT ACHIEVING LEADERSHIP SUCCESS: I recommend you post this self-evaluation someplace where you can see it every day.

Free Git X Bit... For a PDF version of this test, go to www.gitomer.com and enter the words LEADER ATTRIBUTES in the GitBit box.

Are You in Sales, Negotiation, and Mediation? ANSWER: You Bet!

There is an undeniable and ever present need for every leader to be a salesperson, a negotiator, and a mediator.

With all the characteristics required of a leader, you must employ friendly persuasion in order to sell your ideas and convince others that your ideas and your strategies will work.

It's selling in the form of being believable. It's selling in the form of transferring confidence. It's selling in the form of creating an atmosphere where achievement is believable. Any way you look at it – it's sales.

Negotiation is a form of sales. Getting the other person to see it your way and do it your way. Negotiation implies compromise and that can also mean counseling someone else's point of view and modifying your own. But in either event, it's sales.

Mediation is a form of negotiation. But it's between two people – you not being one of them.

You're in the middle, and your job is to resolve the issue to where both people feel that they've won.

My dad taught me the secret of negotiation.

"Son, never offer something you wouldn't take."

-Max Gitomer

Let this advice guide you, as leader, in both negotiation and mediation.

KEY POINT OF UNDERSTANDING: Here are two important philosophies: 1. Your people are not buying your ideas or strategies. They're buying you. The acceptance of you will lead them to your ideas and your strategies. 2. People don't like to be sold, but they love to buy. If your people feel that they're being pushed, their first inclination will be to resist. The secret to sales, especially leadership sales, is to engage by asking questions, rather than trying to convince or coerce by making statements. Once you've mastered these two philosophies, your role as a leader will be forever enhanced.

KEY ACTION TO TAKE: Review your slides and your speeches. Are you engaging by asking, or repelling by telling? Revise at least 30% of your statements into questions, thereby creating dialogue among your team members and perhaps direct interaction with you, and I promise you'll have greater buy in, greater morale, and higher achievement.

Adaptive Leadership

To be a great leader you must have an open, adaptive mind. You must look at each situation, each person, and each task as an opportunity to do better, learn more, and succeed in a way that exceeds your past triumphs, and sets a newer, better reputation in place.

- The older you get, the less you are willing to adapt or change.

- The more experienced you are, the less you are willing to adapt or change.

- The more you drift away from staying a student, the less you are willing to adapt or change.

- The less computer literate you are, the more you fail to recognize the missed opportunities for adapting or changing your philosophy and methodology for leading yourself or others.

Adaptive leadership means taking a situation at hand and creating something better, newer, or more in keeping with the times than what you have been used to doing.

"I've always done it that way" is a phrase you should never think, let alone utter. You've probably always done it that way since before cell phones, or since before the Internet, or laptops, or texting, or social media, or, or, or…

I am certain I have offended some of you talking about how experienced leaders are the last to adapt. Some people refer to it as stubborn, some as hard headed; I refer to it as idiotic and borderline dangerous.

A leader who can't see his or her way clear to seek new strategies, new answers, and new direction based on the times, the people, and the technology needs to quit his or her job and go work at an ostrich farm where everyone's head is already in the sand. They'll feel right at home.

One of the most interesting aspects of being adaptive is that once you start it becomes a never-ending process. It's also much more intellectually challenging, sometimes even much more fun, and clearly, at the end, much more rewarding and much more fulfilling knowing you are a new world leader rather than "sticking to your guns."

Every time I drive to or from the Philadelphia airport I drive by the Philadelphia Navy Yard. There are 100 boats in that naval yard too old to sail, too outdated to battle, too slow to respond, and too dangerous for a sailor to be onboard in the case of an enemy attack. It's referred to as the "Mothball Fleet." A bunch of ships sitting there doing nothing – and because of their age and their limited capability, never will.

They sit, covered in mothballs, because they failed to keep up with the times and technology.

Here are 5.5 things you can do in order to promote your own ability to be more open, to be more current, and to be more adaptive in both your style and your actions:

1. Read more than you watch. A book a month on technology, business, leadership, sales, or psychology will carry you far further than watching television contests, reality shows, reruns, or the local news, or spending an evening at the bar. Dedicate more time to yourself, dedicate more time to your studies, and dedicate more time to reading and learning about what's new.

2. Play more. Play on the Internet for one hour every day. Become an Amazon.com one-click buyer, thus combining your ability to use the Internet with your need to read.

3. Become more attractive. Start a blog. Start a business page on Facebook. Open a Twitter account and tweet your own thoughts and philosophies. You'll know how good they are by how often they get re-tweeted. Get people to follow your thinking by writing and posting your experiences. People will be interested, and join you.

4. Antennas up! Harness the power of observation. Pay attention to, and learn from, everything going on around you. Pay special attention to others who do what you do.

5. Listen with the intent to understand. In other words, don't interrupt until the other person has finished what they are saying; maybe even ask a question rather than simply creating an answer when engaging with others.

5.5 Look in the mirror. Have you become what you set out to become? Are you ecstatic when you look in the mirror? Do you smile and wink at yourself when you look in the mirror? Are your immediate goals posted on the mirror so you can see them and repeat them every day? And finally, how would others rate your ability to adapt?

Because you see, it's not just what you think, it's how others perceive your words, your actions, and your deeds.

KEY POINT OF UNDERSTANDING: Your DESIRE and ABILITY to adapt and accept existing situations AND embrace progress determines your success, and the success of your people.

KEY ACTION TO TAKE: Examine your past 10 decisions. How many of them took into consideration or refused to recognize that the world is different (social media, texting, branding, metrics, Google)? Now reassess those 10 decisions using adaptive skills and see what could have been done different, better, and more collaborative.

The Day TO Day and the Day BY Day.

If you have been a leader for more than five years, you are the most vulnerable to losing your leadership luster.

Even if you don't think you have, I challenge you to read the next pages word-for-word and word-by-word so that you don't fall victim to the trap of apathy and false wisdom.

Many leaders (not you, of course) believe that their knowledge is far superior to that of the people they lead. Many leaders with extended tenure and experience believe they already have the answers and simply wait for circumstances to arise or change.

REALITY: There are three levels of life: groove (in the groove), rut (in a deep groove), grave (in a deep rut). When you begin your career, you are in the groove. Working as hard as you can, working as long as you can, working as smart as you can – and looking to achieve at every opportunity. Time passes. Days become years, and if you try to stay in the same groove it becomes old, it becomes worn, and ultimately it becomes a deeper groove, also known as a rut.

One of the best examples I can give you is your present ability to take advantage of technology, do your own PowerPoint slides, and be the master of your laptop.

And did I mention your inability to acknowledge that Facebook is now one of the three largest countries in the world? You have decided that for one reason or another you don't want to or need to "keep up." You're in a rut.

And then day-by-day you try to hang on and do things the way they've always been done because in just five more years you can retire (or should I say rut-tire).

And the rut deepens to finally become a grave. Don't think of it as dying – think of it as living death by being left behind.

Your job is to STAY IN THE GROOVE. By staying in the groove, you set the example for your people to stay in the groove.

I was asked by a leader, "How do I handle these young kids who have a feeling of entitlement?"

My response was, "You text message them." And the text reads, "There is no entitlement with this job. When you arrive, you'll be working your ass off – and you'll be expected to achieve at a high level." And you send the text to them while they're sitting there in front of you.

If you don't understand that the new generation of employees would rather text than talk, you may be in a rut. If you don't know how to text, you may be in a deep rut.

AUTHOR'S NOTE: I'm trying to teach my grandchildren to text full words (see you tomorrow) instead of text lingo (CU 2mrrw). Are you texting your kids and grandkids?

Staying in the groove means dedicating and re-dedicating yourself to education, excellence, and enthusiasm by example.

KEY POINT OF UNDERSTANDING: If members of your team feel as though they have passed you by or feel as though their skill set is better than your skill set (especially technologically), they will at least resist but most probably rebuke the ideas that you put forward based on the fact that they're no longer applicable in today's world.

KEY ACTION TO TAKE: Improve your computer literacy by 100% within the next 30 days. This means actively learning and becoming proficient at the programs your people use every day. Start a blog. Create some new strategic method of communicating with your people. Take actions that get your team talking about the "new" you. Once you renew your skill set, you will have automatically renewed your ability to influence and inspire.

Sandy Carter Leads From the Front Row.

An hour before my IBM leadership and sales seminar was about to begin, I walked the audience.

Some people came up to greet me and shake my hand, recognizing me or my trademarked maintenance shirt – while others (most of them) glanced at me, assumed I was a maintenance guy, and went about their business as though I was invisible.

The front row of the room was empty save for one person.

"Hi, my name is Jeffrey Gitomer, are you by chance Sandy Carter?" "Yes, I am," she smiled.

We exchanged pleasantries and talked a bit about the event and how excited and honored I was to be presenting.

Sandy Carter, for the uninformed, is an iconic IBM employee. While her official title is Vice President of Software Business Partners & Midmarket, she is unofficially the Queen of Business Social Media. She has been a hands-on, guiding leader inside Big Blue for the past 20 years.

By no coincidence, Sandy selected the front row at my seminar. She tweeted the entire time. And not one person had the confidence or the guts to sit beside her.

I began my talk with a challenge to the audience about their social media presence, and their understanding of the opportunity that social media presents. "How many of you are on LinkedIn?" Almost every hand went up. "How many of you have more than 100 connections?" Half the hands went down. "More than 250 connections?" Almost all the hands went down. "More than 500 connections?" One hand remained in the air. Sandy Carter's.

"How many of you have a Twitter account that you actually use?" A (very) few hands went up. "How many of you have more than 500 Twitter followers?" Three hands. "One thousand followers?" One hand remained in the air. Sandy Carter's. "Five thousand followers?" Carter's hand stayed up. "TEN thousand followers?" Carter's hand stayed up, as the audience gasped.

She's a 20-year, loyal IBM employee. She's responsible for the success of over 1,700 people. She blogs to thousands, tweets to 21,000, and has a LinkedIn connection factor of more than 1,000. She has won 14 marketing innovation awards. And she lives at or near the edge.

She is the classic dictionary definition of "leading by example."

Sandy has written two books (while most leaders are still thinking about theirs). *The New Language of Business: SOA and Web 2.0* and *The New Language of Marketing 2.0*. She'll have her third book written and launched before 99.9% of all other leaders on the planet (with the same amount of tenure) have their first chapter written.

How's your book coming along?

I have decided to use Sandy as an example of leadership because she is IN the fire every day. Her schedule is FULL and her executive assistant Liz is a CLASSIC (no surprise).

Here are a few of the gems from my interview with Sandy (she's electric and you could feel her strength of character and determination on the phone):

PAST HISTORY OF HANDS-ON SUCCESS: "When I approached my first project at IBM in Charlotte, I wanted to differentiate, and I wanted to showcase that I was close with the customer. They asked me to write software for tellers, and I had my differentiating opportunity. I had never been a teller. They were asking me to go out and document teller requirements and talk to them. As I was doing it, I realized that until I actually did it I wouldn't really know what it's like to be a day-to-day teller. So I went out and did an internship at Nation's Bank (NCNB). Hugh McColl, who was also a Harvard grad, let me work at the bank as a teller for two weeks. And let me tell you after two weeks we designed the best teller software ever in the history of IBM.

The development of the software branded me as a rebel in IBM – as someone who listens to the customer. Since that time, I try hard to keep true to 'listening to the customer,' and 20 years later I have discovered that is what social media is all about."

RESULTS FROM TAKING A RISK: "When I tweeted, 'Analytics is the new black,' I was hoping it would get a lot more re-tweets than it did. I did receive a lot of comments on my blog and four or five customers have asked for me to come do briefings with them because they want to understand what social analytics is and what it can do for their company."

TAKING A RISK TO BE FIRST AND WINNING: "When we first started looking at social media, IBM was getting into what I would consider some very cool technology areas. I decided that communicating through social media channels could make us a true technology leader, so I took the plunge. It's working better than I hoped."

LEARNING TO MASTER BEFORE DELEGATING: "I first started leveraging social media personally. I found out how it was allowing me to make connections and have a dialog. As soon as we started the new portfolio as the solution, I instantly added social media into what we were doing to really get the buzz and the energy up. The first thing I did was begin with a blog and then posted a really cool YouTube video."

LEADERSHIP CHALLENGE: "Social media is remarkable. What can happen on Twitter or on a blog can go either good or bad. And as a leader you're very vulnerable. You literally have to be pristine in what you are talking about because someone will take it the wrong way."

LEADERSHIP ACTION: "I want to be an evangelist to my customers and partners. We just did a survey of 3,000 of my partners and we found that 34% are already using social media as a sales tool and the other 66% said 'I haven't started' or 'I have started but I really don't know what I'm doing and I need some education or training.' So we started a series of online training classes and I've done a personal lunch and learn series. Throughout IBM and with my partner community, I can have 3,000 people on a lunch and learn where we go through how to use Twitter, how to create a blog, or how to create links onto Flickr and YouTube. It's pretty amazing how many people are trying to learn. If you don't do it yourself, then you can't teach it."

PHILOSOPHY: *Sandy Carter has a four-part personal and business philosophy of leadership.*

1. *I ensure people push themselves to get the very best out of them.* I know a lot of my team come back and say, "You asked me to do something that I didn't think I could do, and I was mad at you for asking me to do it... and then I did it."

2. *I am personal and personable.* I started a tradition in my last IBM position. I would knit a baby blanket for any person on my team having a baby. Knowing about my team's kids, who has an illness, and who is going through rough times at home, and understanding how much of an impact that makes on performance and relationship, is a treasured characteristic of mine.

3. *I lead by example.* I push myself hard, I work hard, and I believe we are all in the game together – but I want to be the hardest worker among us.

4. *I believe no matter what you're doing, constantly learning and constantly listening will lead you to success.* Someone I really admire at IBM is Steve Mills. He told me that, "Superior skills, and closest to the customer, always wins."

MAKING A DIFFERENCE: Sandy started a super women's group at IBM that is now about 15-16,000 women strong. "What we do is focus on skills like networking, technology, social media, getting together and forming the community, and how to make IBM an even better company and better place for women."

Sandy Carter is a true leader. I have attempted to honor her strategies and achievements, but it would take more than these few pages.

I am challenging you,
the reader, the leader, to
study these accomplishments,
and compare them to yours
over a 20-year period.

After you read her books, follow her on Twitter, and subscribe to her blog, you'll have a better idea of her depth, and the example she is setting globally.

Free GitBit... If you're interested in learning more about Sandy Carter, go to www.gitomer.com and enter the word SANDY in the GitBit box.

STRENGTH

5

COACH
LEADERSHIP

The strength to learn
coaching skills in order to
support, train, and encourage
each team member to
achievement and victory.

Are You a Leader or a Coach? YES!

So you're a leader. You have a team of people – and you have goals, projects, tasks, and challenges.

Big deal. So do a lot of people.

THE QUESTION IS: How good are you?

Not how good are your people – how good are *you?*

How do you consistently exceed your goals, have no turnover, inspire your people to be their best, have buy-in from upper management on all your new ideas, and still have time to play with your cat?

First, ask yourself how you became a leader. Were you a top-notch employee who was promoted because of your achievements? Were you one of the only people on the team who had some leadership experience? Or were you recruited and hired to come in and turn things around?

However you got the title, it is your job to make an impact while you are in this position, and to set a new standard for excellence that future leaders will need to live up to.

In my experience, it's easier and more understandable to coach people to success than to lead people to success.

One of the first things I would want to know as a new leader would be the best month or year (however these things are measured) in the history of the company. My initial goal would be to surpass that mark, and that is a goal I would share with all the members of my team. Meet with them and explain your dual role of leader and coach. Tell them as a leader, you'll give them directions – and as a coach, you'll teach them how and encourage them to win.

You need to gain the trust and confidence of all members of the team. This is best accomplished by meeting with them, going out with them on appointments, and having as much face-to-face dialog with them as possible.

As a leader, your people want to perform for you. Your job is to coach them to a winning performance.

KEY POINT OF UNDERSTANDING: Most people have had a coach that influenced them way beyond the game. If you had one (and I hope you did), emulate those inspiring skills and you'll achieve the same influence, impact, and outcome.

KEY ACTION TO TAKE: After you give yourself an HONEST self-assessment, find a coach and ask them if you can pay them for their help. Let him or her embrace and encourage you to greater discipline and improved skills so that you can in turn "pass it on."

Put Me In, Coach!

Put me in, coach! Put me in, coach! Put me in, coach! Put me in, coach!

Those are words ALWAYS spoken with enthusiasm and passion. That's what your players want! They want to be in the game. They are eager to play for you. And they want to be coached to victory.

I want to challenge you to stop managing your people and start leading them by coaching them.

A coach is a person who can also DO whatever he tells others to do.

Here are 14.5 personal attributes and qualities that make a coach a winning coach:

1. **You have valuable information that people can use.**

2. **You combine your experience with the real world.**

3. **You have a sense of humor.**

4. **You know the game better than they do.**

5. **You encourage.**

6. **You are a great presenter.**

7. **You have standards and ethics that you follow, not just preach.**

8.   You are enthusiastic.

9.   You have great communication skills.

10. Your players like you.

11. Your players believe in you.

12. You inspire others.

13. You tell the truth all the time.

14. Your players respect you.

14.5 You can play.

Think about some of the most famous coaches of all time. They are also among the most revered and the most respected people of all time. Knute Rockne, Vince Lombardi, John Wooden, Joe Paterno, Don Shula. These are people who inspired a team of winners. And so can you.

Here are 20.5 elements of coaching greatness to master:

1. IT'S EASIER TO TRAIN A SMART PERSON THAN AN IDIOT.
Hire smart people.

2. IT'S POSSIBLE TO TRAIN A HAPPY PERSON. It's impossible to train an unhappy person. Hire happy people.

Pretty simple so far huh? It gets harder from here on.

3. HOW GOOD YOU ARE DETERMINES HOW WILLING THEY ARE TO LEARN FROM YOU. Get great at every skill and make tough plays in front of your people.

4. "BY EXAMPLE" IS THE ONLY WAY. Don't tell them what to do. Show them how it's done.

5. ROLE-PLAY REALISTICALLY. Role-play with employees, vendors, salespeople, sales managers, and with customers. You can actually role-play with your best customer. You can't get more real world than that.

6. TEACH YOUR PEOPLE, ESPECIALLY YOUR SALESPEOPLE, HOW TO HELP AND HOW TO GIVE VALUE. If you're a sales leader, don't just teach selling skills; teach buying motives. Remember my sales mantra: *People don't like to be sold, but they love to buy.* The customer wants to know how they can produce more and profit more.

7. BENCHMARK REAL ANSWERS AND BEST ANSWERS. You haven't encountered any new problems in 20 years. Maybe 50. List every problem that occurs and then determine your best response for each of those situations. Teach your people best responses.

8. HAVE A CONTEST THAT ANYONE CAN WIN. Not just the most sales, how about most referrals or fewest complaints – or most dollars collected, the most new accounts, the most renewed accounts, the most improved person, the highest percentage of account increase, or the fewest service calls. Make them contests that give real incentive. And don't be cheap with the prizes. Give your people things they want, but might never buy themselves.

9. AWARD ACHIEVEMENT IN PUBLIC. And don't be stingy with praise, plaques, or prizes. Awards create job pride, and incentive to achieve.

10. SUPPORT YOUR TEAM EFFORT WITH PROMOTIONS, PRODUCTS, AND PEOPLE. If you want your sales team to win, you and everyone in the company have to be behind them, supporting them. When they're out in the field don't let them feel alone.

11. TEACH YOUR PEOPLE TO NETWORK OUTSIDE THE NORMAL SALES BARRIERS. Informal and casual business beats formal business any day. Your people need to go to meetings where customers and prospects go, and get to know them personally.

12. TEACH YOUR PEOPLE THE SCIENCE OF ASKING QUESTIONS. If you ask smart questions, they think you're smart. If you ask dumb questions, they think you're dumb. Make sure your people ask the most powerful question of all – make sure they ask for the sale or a commitment every time they go to a customer.

13. TEACH YOUR PEOPLE AND YOURSELF TO BE CREATIVE. A creative sales call means you walk in with ideas and answers on how to help your customer produce more and profit more. If you walk in with information about you, they consider you a salesman; if you walk in with ideas and answers, they consider you a resource. Here's the problem: Ideas and answers require preparation. Here's the good news: Your people's ability to bring creative ideas to the table will be the difference between getting the business and losing the business. And here's the secret: Creativity is a science. You can learn it. Start with a book called *Thinkertoys* by Michael Michalko.

14. PAY MORE FOR OUTSIDE TRAINING. Outside training will present new perspectives and eliminate political hierarchies and agendas from overtaking outcomes. It will keep your mind open to new ideas and concepts, as well as to new strategies and methodologies that will help you and your people get better.

15. WHEN YOU TEACH YOUR PEOPLE, TEACH THEM AN EQUAL AMOUNT OF SALES SKILLS, PRESENTATION SKILLS, AND PERSONAL DEVELOPMENT SKILLS. Selling skills and buying motives are only a third of the equation. Presentation skills allow the message to be delivered with passion, and personal development skills determine the attitude and enthusiasm by which you present. Here's a hint: Personal development skills (like attitude, goal setting, and listening) were never taught in school. They are courses you gotta teach yourself and master yourself. If you want to know the real secret, the best way to master them is to teach them.

16. TRAIN YOUR PEOPLE AND YOURSELF EVERY DAY. Even if it's only 15 minutes a day. One new lesson a day will give you 250 new ideas and strategies a year.

17. ESTABLISH AN AGENDA FOR YOUR WEEKLY STAFF MEETING AND STICK TO IT. Make the meeting fun. Don't make it all about what's wrong. Make it all about what's right. And make certain that it contains five times more real information, positive news, and training than it does administrivia (stuff you could have e-mailed).

18. LISTEN TO CDs AND READ BOOKS EVERY DAY. Many of your people are in the car driving from job to job or commuting. Their automobiles (or public transportation) should be a university. They should be listening to new ideas and personal development strategies so that when they get to work they're energized and charged up with new information. The best way to master any skill, especially a business skill, is to try it out the minute you learn it.

19. RECORD YOURSELF. Record your notes after you attend a seminar, record yourself reading a book, record the promises you make to others, record your presentations, record your training sessions. Then watch them or listen to them. What you see and hear will reveal who you really are vs. who you think you are. Recording is the best/only way to know where you are and what to improve.

20. STAY TEACHABLE AND COACHABLE YOURSELF. The more you study it, the better you'll be at teaching it. The more you coach it, the better you'll master it.

20.5 HARNESS THE POWER OF ENCOURAGEMENT. Encouragement is the best way to get results. Yelling and threatening will breed resentment and ultimately create turnover. Encouragement will create pride and self-assurance and also generate more business.

If you're looking for a report card – just look at the number of people that turn over in your organization. If the number is high then your ability to coach is probably low.

KEY POINT OF UNDERSTANDING: If you've ever played sports, you will always remember the coach you really loved. He or she is the one you still stay in touch with. The one you report your progress to. The one you want to be proud of you. How many of your past employees stay in touch with you?

Coaching is not easy. That's what makes it so rewarding. And your ability to coach, better stated, your ability to master the science of coaching will be in direct proportion to how many games, *how many business games*, you and your people win.

KEY ACTION TO TAKE: Allocate time each day (even if it's just an hour) to work on one personal attribute of a winning coach or one element of coaching greatness. Implement or take action on a best practice. This accomplishes two things: 1. You improve. 2. You document a strategy of replication that can help your people improve. The old adage is, "If you want your people to get better, you have to get better." That adage is old because it's true.

One Coach's Opinion.

Lee Corso is one of the all-time "most losses" coaches in the history of Indiana football.

His record over his 10-year stint was 41–68–2. He is currently a sports broadcaster and football analyst for ESPN. He is engaging and funny, and he uses himself as an example of coaching. Is he a winner or loser? You tell me.

He gave a speech today. The people in his audience, many of them business leaders, were looking for a way to get from managing and leading to coaching.

Corso used the model of how to coach to transfer his message of how to lead. And even though he was a losing coach, he ended up a winner and so did many of his players.

I began writing as fast as I could. I wanted to capture the essence of his message and how that might relate to me, and you. Extracted from my two pages of notes, here are the learning points I felt were most impactful. All of them will make you think about (and perhaps re-think) your own leadership coaching strategies and actions.

1. Coach against excellence. With excellence as a model and a goal, winning becomes more habitual. Too many players strive to win the game rather than be their best. Reverse the model and you have the formula for success. First be excellent, and then become a winner.

2. Coach to win, not to make money. If you win, the money will follow. The best model is always to play to be your best and do your best. Somehow the best players always end up with the most money. They become winners because they think like winners and play like winners.

3. Leaders are not always responsible for the outcomes of their players, but they are always accountable for them. Coaches are measured by the success of their team. It's too bad this is the measuring stick because great coaches are not always as successful in the win/loss arena as they are in the building character arena. Corso was a great coach, but he lost too many games. The end result was that they found another coach. Corso went on to fame and fortune – and no one knows the name of the person they replaced him with.

4. Leaders are cool, not cold. If it's not working out between you and one of your players, you don't cut them. You ask them, "How do you want to handle it?" You transfer the responsibility and even the decision to the other person.

5. Prejudice and disloyalty will equal destruction. If you want your people to be loyal to you, first you must be loyal to them. Same with your customers. You can't get loyalty until you give loyalty. When loyalty erodes, the foundation crumbles. Just look at any professional sport. No one is loyal to anyone anymore. The fans don't matter and they're the ones providing the revenue. Teams aren't loyal to players. Players aren't loyal to teams or fans. Look at professional baseball or any professional sport and you can see that greed has overtaken the sense of doing the right thing.

6. With recognition comes responsibility. As you become better known as a coach, your responsibility to exceed your best increases. The opposite of responsibility is blame. Great coaches praise their players in a winning effort and take responsibility for the loss in a losing effort.

7. Let people create their own fortunes. In a Chinese fortune cookie you randomly select what someone else has written. Make your own fortune cookies. Create your own fortunes by writing them down instead of reading what someone else has written.

8. Earn money by not going for the money. Help other people, give value to other people, and you'll earn all the money in the world.

One of the most interesting things about Corso's talk was the environment in which it was delivered. A business development breakfast club. Lots of networking, lots of prospecting, lots of interacting with existing customers and future customers, and lots of meeting new people. In short, lots of excitement. Possibly the best business building networking opportunity that I've seen.

By the time Lee Corso took the stage everyone was ready, primed, and eager to hear his message. In part because of his celebrity status, but also because people were eager to learn.

As a result, his message was very transferable. Everyone laughed at the funny parts, and learned at the salient parts. Personally, I have implemented several of his ideas.

If you've ever played sports, you had a coach. Little league, soccer, high school, and college. That coach impacted your success. I find it more than interesting that once people get their business cards printed the coach is gone.

As a leader or an employer, your biggest responsibility is to coach and encourage your people to succeed. Coach them to be excellent. Coach them to score. Coach them to win.

If you're a salesperson or businessperson, seek a coach. Find someone that can teach you advanced fundamentals, offer you sound advice, and encourage you to win.

When I talk to athletes they'll often tell me they stay in touch with their favorite coach, or they went back to visit their old coach. The reason they do it is because they want to brag to their coach about how good they've become. Bragging may not be the best word – maybe pride would serve as a better word. But the bottom line is they went back and sought this coach out because he or she was so influential in their earlier lives.

Who comes back to visit you? If your past employees are calling you on the phone and thanking you for the lessons, thanking you for the opportunities, thanking you for the foundation you provided them, then your coaching prowess has been affirmed. If they're not calling you, perhaps you need to find your own coach.

A coach is someone who tells you what you don't want to hear, who has you see what you don't want to see, so you can be who you have always known you could be.

— *Tom Landry*

Dealing With Winners, Losers, and Mediocres.

Everyone loves a winner. One of the most overlooked aspects of a leader's time management (which I refer to as time allocation) is how much time they spend on losers and mediocres and fail to invest in winners.

It's critical for you as a leader to invest time in those who you believe can help the most, produce the most, and achieve the most. Let go of the losers and encourage the mediocres in proportion to the time that you invest in the winners.

General Electric became one of the most successful and profitable companies in the world by eliminating their bottom 10% of performers annually. While this may seem a little harsh, I can promise you the incentive for mediocre performers is high.

Don't leave your winners alone. Meet with them. Challenge them. Encourage them. And collaborate with them to help them achieve at a higher level.

Make certain the latest tools of technology are at their disposal and that they have complete freedom to act within your boundaries and set their own pace to win.

My experience has shown me that winners start earlier and finish later than losers and mediocres.

Low-end performers arrive at work "on time" and greet the winners who are already seated at their desks, already on fire.

KEY POINT OF UNDERSTANDING: You have a finite number of hours in your day. How you choose to allocate them will not only determine productivity, but also achievement. Focus on your best people and invest most of your time with them. Coach them and let them know your appreciation, and praise them as much as you guide them, delegate to them, and challenge them. The rest of your team will try harder to get to that inner circle.

KEY ACTION TO TAKE: Identify the characteristics of each winner on your team. Meet with them to gain a clear understanding of what makes them achieve. By doing this, you may actually be helping them understand why they're a winner themselves for the first time. You may also find that the majority of your winners have many of the same characteristics – not just an inner drive or an inner fire, but also a deep belief and love for what they do and a service heart for why they do it. Take this information and begin to share it in bits and pieces with those that are striving to be winners but aren't quite there yet.

Team or Family?

Whenever I ask a leader how many people are in their group, they will respond with a number and the word team. "I have 17 people on my team."

Sometimes they will say, "I am responsible for a team of 21." I always like when a leader includes the word responsible in any statement because it indicates their thinking – and how they view their role as leader. A responsible leader.

I've been a business owner since the late 1960s. I've always considered myself a businessman rather than an entrepreneur. Probably because my dad was a businessman and my mom was a businesswoman, and most of our family friends were businesspeople. They all owned or operated "family businesses."

As a result of those exposures, I've always considered my business a family business, and have always had members of my family involved in the business. I never felt that I had a team of people; I had (and still have) a family.

I don't know of many leaders or business owners who define it this way. But I have found that by using "family thinking" rather than team thinking it's a much more personal business, and I tend to take more family actions than corporate actions.

Here are 4.5 examples of "family thinking" in my business:

1. Benefits are based on what I would provide for my family.
Health and dental insurance is provided. AAA Roadside Assistance is provided. Life insurance is provided. These are the same benefits I would give my children, so I give them to the rest of the family.

2. Everyone eats.
When you go to the refrigerator in your home, you don't leave a dollar for a soda. You just take it. It's the same in my business. Food is free. And not just for our family – also for the family of people that service us. The copier repair person, the FedEx delivery person, and the plant lady. They all know there's food at Buy Gitomer that they're more than welcome to partake of.

3. Family celebrations.
Birthdays and special occasions create opportunities for the family to gather (many are in separate offices all day) and have pizza or sandwiches to celebrate. It's a relaxed time where people get to know each other as human beings, not just as co-workers.

4. Living benefits.
Every employee is entitled to a free health club membership at the local YMCA. This serves two purposes. First is the opportunity for everyone in the company to get healthy or stay healthy. And second it's part of my ongoing commitment to help the city of Charlotte.

4.5 The atmosphere is relaxed.
We're not a PC-company. People are responsible for their own productivity. People are responsible for their own hours. And people are responsible for their own tasks – without language or protocol getting in the way.

KEY POINT OF UNDERSTANDING: Whether you call your people a team or a family, as a leader you have a responsibility to create the internal atmosphere in your office or at your place of business. And I maintain that in a relaxed atmosphere, where people feel at home and can grab something to eat when they're hungry, great morale and high productivity follow suit.

KEY ACTION TO TAKE: Assess the current condition of the people on your team. How do you think they feel about coming to work every day? And how do they interact with others? Ask yourself if there's something you could do that would improve their feelings about the business and increase their productive time while they're in your office or theirs. WARNING: You may have to spend a few more dollars to make this happen, but I promise you those dollars are well invested.

Some People Want a Team, Some People Don't.

Leaders have a group of people that they're responsible for. And while they all work for the same group or the same company, they may not look at themselves as team members. They view themselves as individuals who work for the company, but may not necessarily want to work with others.

Salespeople are always referred to as a team. But the reality is they don't play well with others. They're actually competing against one another to see who can be best, and secretly hoping that the person working next to them quits, get fired, or dies so they can have the other guy's accounts. People in IT rarely sit around the campfire to roast marshmallows together. Rather, they come to work with a set of headphones and rarely socialize with others.

KEY POINT OF UNDERSTANDING: Leadership thinking revolves around how you and your people feel about what's taking place. Counsel their opinions. Leadership action revolves around how you expect each individual to perform and produce a desired end result.

KEY ACTION TO TAKE: Obviously team strength is better than a bunch of individuals. Teams of dogs win races; cats don't play well together. If you have a bunch of dogs and cats on your team (and maybe a few mules), identify them and assign tasks accordingly.

STRENGTH

6

(The New) SITUATIONAL LEADERSHIP

The strength and understanding to separate task from person, and to identify how ready, willing, and able each team member is to accept tasks enthusiastically, and to always give and do their best.

Hersey Situational Leadership® Model Situational Leadership 2010-2020

By: Paul "Doc" Hersey and Ron Campbell

AUTHOR'S NOTE: I am including the Hersey Situational Leadership® Model because it is the best (by far) task-oriented process for achievement. The majority of this book is about "you" the leader, not the follower or "it" the task. But the fact is they are all connected. The Center for Leadership Studies and the Paul Hersey team agree with my thinking and have provided a glimpse of the successful relationship between you the leader, the follower, and the task. I am honored to include it, and I urge you to take advantage of it.

It would be great to sit with you, to share the Hersey Model one-on-one. As you read this, think of those times when your leadership just worked, when you were in the "leadership zone." The Hersey Model was built to help you quickly find that zone.

There's a reason the Model has lasted for decades and resonated with tens of millions of leaders around the world: *it makes sense, it's easy to understand and apply, and IT WORKS!* The Model reflects best practices of real leaders, and it is rich in skills that can be easily learned and used daily to achieve success.

NOTE: The Hersey Situational Leadership® Model is based on sound research and decades of success stories. Feel free to contact the Center for Leadership Studies and we will be happy to share the research that contributed to the development of the model. (You can find us on the web at www.situational.com or by calling 866-545-4951.)

To properly align with this book, the emphasis of this lesson will stay on you – on what happens in that moment of influence. How do you quickly read the situation and accurately assess the other person's ability to successfully perform? What influence behaviors must you need to help them to succeed?

Here are three learnable skills to master:

SKILL ONE: IDENTIFY A SPECIFIC TASK.

Deciding and defining what it is that needs to get done. Part of this skill of defining what needs to get done is communicating it in a way that the follower understands what it is that you want. We often hear people express this as "getting on the same page" or "having the same picture."

HERE'S AN EXAMPLE: You've identified that the TASK is to write a proposal to a client. Let's take a member of your team, Pat. Pat has just excitedly approached you. It is her client that has requested a written proposal. This proposal is not too time sensitive and Pat has previously expressed a desire to learn this skill.

What we have here is a great opportunity to grow Pat's abilities and keep her highly engaged.

SKILL TWO: DIAGNOSING THE FOLLOWER'S PERFORMANCE NEEDS FOR THAT TASK.

The question is: How ready is Pat for writing this proposal? You don't really have to be precise. Ratings like low, moderate, or high are very good benchmarks. BE AWARE: It's important to understand that whatever readiness decision you make about Pat writing this proposal, it will only count for this proposal. Take another task of hers – client interactions or account management – and you have an entirely different diagnosis.

Readiness switches from task to task, even moment to moment. Just because someone gets to high levels of performance for one task, does not mean they stay there for the next. An e-mail or phone call can change how ready a person is. Co-worker interactions, family problems, or a child's health can affect their performance. It's easy to see how this distraction may very well impact a person's ability – even their willingness – to focus on the task at hand.

Always diagnose in the here and now. You can make sound decisions about what they need from you to perform at this moment, and be flexible if conditions or circumstances change.

SKILL THREE: APPLYING THE BEST COMBINATION OF TASK AND RELATIONSHIP LEADER BEHAVIORS.

This is the key to successful outcomes. Take this third skill apart, word for word.

Start with *applying*. The Hersey Situational Leadership® Model focuses on behavior and not intent. So this third skill is all about how well you use – or apply – your behaviors to impact the other person's ability to perform.

Combination is a mix, a blend of Task and Relationship Behaviors. While not leaving one out, you may use low to high amounts of each independently to create the best combination.

Task Behavior is how much, who, what, when, where, and how you "need" to provide in order for the follower to perform. (Pay special attention to the word need in that previous sentence.) *Relationship Behavior* is two-way communication, praise, encouragement, talking about why, proclaiming, or building trust. The decision is about selecting which type of relationship behavior will be most meaningful to the follower for this task.

Let's apply this to Pat and writing the proposal. Since this is her first one, you'll need to provide the what, when, and how. (High amounts of Task Behavior.) There will be explanations of why that will need to be provided. Pat will have questions so there will be a significant amount of two-way communication. With a bit of encouragement from you, the learning will be engaging. (High amounts of Relationship Behavior.)

HERE'S ANOTHER EXAMPLE: Pat has walked into your office and asked if you have a moment for her. A client just called Pat and demanded a complete change to their ordering process. The change is critical to them, and they need the change done before noon the next day. Pat knows their process well.

Here is how to use all three skills in harmony for this example:

SKILL ONE: IDENTIFY THE TASK.

Change an ordering process for a client.

SKILL TWO: DIAGNOSING.

Pat knows the client's current process very well. She has also worked on two similar changes recently, and both were accomplished to the specs and on time. She has the skills to make the change. Frankly, you are surprised by Pat's reaction and ask her, "Pat, what is it about this change that you find challenging?" She responds, "The time!"

SKILL THREE: APPLYING THE BEST COMBINATION OF TASK AND RELATIONSHIP LEADER BEHAVIORS.

Pat does not require step-by-step direction to get the changes done. She has previously demonstrated the skill. The leader's (your) question was a great start in using Relationship Behavior to influence Pat. If the leader continues with the questioning (High Relationship): *Is this any more complicated than the other two you did so well on? How much time will this one take? How much time did the previous two take? Do you need any backup resources? Do we need a plan B?"*

If the answers to these questions come from Pat, she will come to realize she can handle this and the leader will be able to delegate. (Low Relationship and Low Task.) If Pat cannot answer the questions and does not respond with a little encouragement (High Relationship and Low Task), the leader can become more involved and provide some structure for meeting the deadline (High Task and High Relationship). One of the great things about the Hersey Situational Leadership® Model is how fluid and responsive you can be to follower needs. This is leadership in the moment.

So what does it take to achieve effective influence and task completion with a positive outcome?

The answer is as simple as applying the Hersey Situational Leadership® Model with a Resilient Attitude! Leadership is about your ability to work through others to get things done successfully. It's just as important to keep those individuals positively connected to you as the leader and the organization – this is where having a resilient attitude and resilient stature is important to outcome. It is a leader's responsibility to not only get things done successfully, but also to keep their followers engaged, ready, and eager for the next task. That's the value of leadership.

NEW FINDINGS: Adding YES! Attitude and leadership resilience to the Hersey Situational Leadership® Model elevates the process for the next decade to the NEW Situational Leadership 2010-2020. These two elements give the existing Situational Leader and the new Situational Leader a competitive advantage and a winning advantage.

Ready, Willing, Able, Best

Every single leader considers himself or herself to be ready, willing, and able. And every leader wants their people or team members to be ready, willing, and able. If I ask you if you are ready, willing, and able – you would most likely answer, "yes."

Some of you would even answer emphatically, "YES!"

NOTE: There's a catch. Although people, both leaders and followers, are ready, willing, and able – there's no guarantee that they're going to give it their all when assigned a task or given an opportunity to perform.

One of the most interesting aspects and one of the most unspoken parts of action and/or doing is the desire, *your* desire, to do everything full force. Better stated, to do everything at the level of "best."

Small tasks, big tasks, competitive tasks, active tasks, and passive tasks all have to have (at the end of the task) the word BEST, and your thought of, "I did my best."

Ever been to a restaurant (or a place of business) where you received lousy service, and after you complained, the person serving you said, "I am doing the best I can"? And your thought process said, "Are you kidding me?"

When someone says they are doing the best they can it usually means the opposite, doesn't it?

It is better never to SAY, "I am doing the best I can." Rather, just DO the best you can, and you will never have to say it, the result will speak for itself.

The word BEST is very difficult to define in writing, but it's easy to react to and easy to feel when you are doing it. It's a personal dedication, and a work ethic, not a word.

After EVERY base-on-balls (walk), baseball immortal Pete Rose RAN to first base. The ONLY ballplayer to ever do so. All 1566 times he walked, he ran. That's BEST. Oh, he also had 4256 hits, and was known for his head-first slide to stretch a single to a double. He also holds the all-time record for doubles. No coincidence.

No matter where you are on the food chain of leadership or followership, best is not an option. Best is a way of life. It starts with best thinking.

In leadership, best is also an example that you set for others. Your people will perform to your level of best as much as they will to their level of best.

Michael Jordan owns the Charlotte Bobcats NBA team. He sits at the end of the bench during every single game. How do you think his players feel about giving and doing their best knowing that the guy at the end of the bench is arguably THE best? Do you think it raises their level of play?

Who's sitting at the end of your bench? Who is raising your level of play? Who is inspiring you to play your best? And what are you doing about it?

KEY POINT OF UNDERSTANDING: People doing their best are obvious, and equally obvious are people not doing their best. No matter where you are on the food chain of leadership or followership, best is not an option. Best is a way of life. It starts with best thinking.

KEY ACTION TO TAKE: Over the course of the next 30 days, assign every task and make every delegation to the person who you consider to be best for that task. This will be difficult to do because there are often other pressures and internal politics that will challenge this process, but by selecting your best people you assure yourself that the measurement of the completion and the ultimate outcome of each task will be at its highest level. It will also make evident who your prime players are and who needs to be demoted to the minor leagues.

Personal Enthusiasm and Task Enthusiasm.

Once you understand that an enthusiastic person may not be so enthusiastic about the task given to them, you come to the realization that there's a difference, a big difference, between an enthusiastic person and their willingness to be equally enthusiastic about the task you've delegated, the assignment you've given, or the rule you've handed down.

Thirty five years ago, when I heard Earl Nightingale tell me that enthusiasm came from the Greek word "entheos" (which means "the god within"), I changed my entire thought process by realizing that I create my own enthusiasm, and that I cannot rely on things or other people to create it for me.

Your job as leader is to teach that same lesson to all of your people so that they might receive the same gift. A gift that altered my internal enthusiasm for the better, forever.

KEY POINT OF UNDERSTANDING: Enthusiasm is contagious. Either by presence or by absence. The more enthusiastic you are as a leader, the more enthusiastic it's likely your people will be – and the more ready and willing they will be to accept whatever task you give them.

KEY ACTION TO TAKE: Become enthusiastic first. Combine this with your positive attitude, your YES! Attitude, your compelling presentation skills, and your people will be more receptive, more productive, and feel better about themselves.

STRENGTH 7

MEASUREMENT LEADERSHIP

The strength to make
certain that you measure
performance and outcome
for self-improvement,
and team improvement.

Sales Leaders are the Classic Example of Measured Results.

For more than 20 years, I've been directly involved with the most results-driven and results-measured group of leaders. They're the men and women who lead teams of salespeople.

They have the most "results" pressure. There's executive leadership from above, ordering them to sell more, sell more, sell more. There's pressure to provide new revenue so that their companies may profit and prosper. And there's pressure from below to lead and encourage their teams of sales performers so they can meet or exceed their sales goals, in order that the goals of their companies can be met and plans can be executed.

When you think about the quote, "Nothing happens until a sale is made," then you understand the real need for execution by the sales leader AND the ultimate measurement of their every action and result.

It never ceases to amaze me that CEOs of giant corporations, who get interviewed on major talk shows, never even acknowledge (let alone thank) their salespeople or their sales leaders for the hard work that they've done to make that CEO's appearance possible.

KEY POINT OF UNDERSTANDING: Not all leadership is clearly measured. And not all leaders want to be measured. If you apply the lessons from sales and sales leadership, you will be able to uncover aspects of your leadership, your tasks, and your goals that can be measured and should be measured – not just as a report card of your team, but also as an obvious report card of your present capability.

KEY ACTION TO TAKE: If you're looking to measure the results of your leadership, find a sales leader in your company (or in any company) and talk to them about how they hire, how they train, how they educate, how they set goals, how they achieve goals, how they celebrate their successes, and of course how they measure every aspect of their process and performance.

Measuring Results

My online training company uses the Kirkpatrick Scale to measure training results. For large corporate customers who want ROI combined with measurement, we use Jack Phillips' Five Level ROI Method. The first four levels are Kirkpatrick, and the fifth (Phillips) is ROI – where we tie the post training behavior change and results to the financial metrics we have agreed on and baselined with the customer.

Measurement against training outcomes is no longer an option.

The four levels of Kirkpatrick's training (learning) evaluation model essentially measure:

- **Reaction of student.** What they thought and felt about the training.

- **Learning.** The resulting increase in knowledge or capability.

- **Behavior.** Extent of behavior and capability improvement and implementation/application.

- **Results.** The effects on the business or environment resulting from the trainee's performance.

All Kirkpatrick's measurements are recommended for full and meaningful evaluation of learning in organizations, although their application can increase the complexity of measurement, and usually cost, through the levels of the learning and implementation process.

Some things are easy to measure. Was the task done on time? Was it done correctly? Was the quality of workmanship perfect? And what were the associated costs, or even return on investment? What was the profitability?

But there is way more to measurement than the Kirkpatrick scale and the Jack Phillips 5 Level ROI Model. Especially as you seek to measure task outcome and employee performance.

As a leader, your job is to measure the intangibles as well:

- **Was the result what I expected?**
- **Was the task completed on time?**
- **How did the people on the task respond?**
- **How did the people on the task perform?**
- **Was it a valuable use of our time?**
- **Was it a valuable use of my time?**
- **Should we continue?**
- **Should we do this again?**
- **What did we learn?**
- **Was it worth it?**

- **How cooperative were the people?**

- **How did they feel once the task was completed?**

- **How did this task help them learn more?**

- **How did this task help in their career advancement?**

- **What was each person's fulfillment factor?**

- **How well did my team cooperate and collaborate with one another to complete this task?**

Free Git Bit... If you'd like my succinct (but certainly incomplete) list of measurement scales and devices you can use, go to www.gitomer.com and enter the word MEASUREMENT in the GitBit box.

KEY POINT OF UNDERSTANDING: Measuring is not just the Kirkpatrick scale, or loop, or an ROI. It's also your simple task of writing, "What did we do?" and "How did we do?" and "What happened as a result?" NOTE WELL: Measurement has as much to do with outcome (results, morale, impact) as it does investment. What happened and what new opportunities did the outcome create?

KEY ACTION TO TAKE: Create a list of questions that add YOUR measurement to each task, project, or event. Review those answers and results with the key individuals involved and make improvement plans accordingly.

Measuring Yourself: The 360 Strategy. Smart or Du... er, Less Than Perfect?

From a conceptual perspective, the 360 assessment seems phenomenal. As a leader, you leave yourself open to feedback, both good and bad, both practical and impractical, both docile and hostile, both complimentary and insulting. It's supposed to be an improvement opportunity, and a core process of today's business and government.

ON THE SURFACE: 360 allows everyone on a team or in a company complete communication, and an avenue for the leader to react and respond. It also gives the leader the opportunity to give his or her people the same feedback and get their response.

UNDER THE SURFACE: I would like to have 10 cents for every 360 assessment or document that was never acted upon once completed. With that thin dime, I would become a multi-millionaire. I would have won the lottery.

SITUATION: Many leaders become defensive when their abilities are challenged. Other leaders are accepting, but do nothing about it – unwilling to change, unwilling to move. And still others are resentful that they even have to go through the process.

A small percentage of those assessed are accepting and responsive. They have a willingness to improve AND take action to prove their willingness.

I don't know the exact percentage, but neither does anyone else. And if some big company says they do, they're guessing.

SMART 360: Susan Cordts, President and CEO of Adaptive Technologies, Inc., has created a complete assessment PROCESS that can actually make traditional 360 work. And interesting enough, she calls it, "Smart 360." For the first time it ties all the responses in the 360 assessment, both good and bad, to a corresponding training program. This may seem obvious to you, but at present it's non-existent in all other 360 assessments.

There's one other major challenge that seems to be a common thread throughout this book: The percentage of 360 respondents willing to take action on their challenges would go up tenfold if they were all willing to take a positive attitude course prior to reading the reports.

REALITY: 360 is not an assessment – it's a strategy. Once the assessment is completed, ACTION is necessary. Achievement and improvement actions. Are you among the willing?

Free GitBit... If you'd like to know more about how Smart 360 works, go to www.gitomer.com and enter the words SMART 360 in the GitBit box – or visit Susan's website at www.adaptiveinc.com.

STRENGTH

8

OPPORTUNITY
LEADERSHIP

The strength to
recognize "change" as
"opportunity" – and
the vision to take
advantage of it.

Crisis is the Best Time to Effect Change.

What's happening in your personal world?
What's happening in your business world?
What's happening in your leadership world?

Change is in the air. You can feel it like a crisp fall day. You can almost smell it.

THE QUESTION IS: How will you react to that change?

THE BIGGER QUESTION IS: Do you understand that change is opportunity?

THE BIGGEST QUESTION IS: How will you take advantage of that opportunity?

We are in a crisis. Some will define it in other words, like recession or downturn, but the actions we as a people and a government take over the next few months will shape our world for the next decade.

Some people are "waiting to see what happens." Big mistake. There are three kinds of people – people who make things happen, people who watch things happen, and people who don't know what's happening. Which kind are you?

TAKE NOTE: You can't change things in THE world, but you can change things in YOUR world.

Now is the perfect time to change your situation, and take a greater "self-leadership" position. Now is the perfect time to take control of yourself – your thoughts, your expressions, and your actions.

If you're leading a team of salespeople (also known as revenue generators), now is the time to encourage them to SELL – to sell better and with more passion than ever before. Have your salespeople start with existing customers. Serve them so phenomenally that they buy more, and refer you to others. That's not a change you can "live with" – that's a change you can survive with, even thrive with. Don't just guard your desk and your job. Guard your customers. They are your lifeblood.

REALITY: In order to change whatever you were doing before, you must intensify your efforts.

TRANSLATION: In order to effect that change, work harder and smarter than ever before, and do it with a positive attitude and a service heart.

HERE'S THE SECRET: Outside change makes inside change okay.

At this moment, many people in our society are looking for answers – or, better stated, WAITING for answers.

What are you waiting for?
What are you looking for?
What are you doing?

While this time is passing there are three atmospheres:

- **One is fear and anger.** Being bitter, not better.
- **One is hope and anxiousness.** Waiting instead of doing.
- **One is positive anticipation and determination.** Digging in and doing.

Which atmosphere do you exist in?

HOPE: As I travel across the United States, I've noticed there is a renewed sense of friendliness and patriotism. A sense of union I've never witnessed. There is a willingness among many to try to get better and work harder. And clearly, there is a renewed sense of urgency.

Yes, there's fear, frustration, and disappointment. But not as much as you might read about or hear about. (**HINT:** They rarely show the good things on TV.) The key is to not be angry about it. Anger affects your attitude, your ability to think clearly and think creatively, and your ability to see the best answers and the best opportunity for you.

Sure, you want to be safe, but consider those who pay you, those you serve, and those around you. They are affected too. And their response to the same situation will most likely be different than yours.

PROBLEM: Big companies are looking to remain profitable. They are doing it at the expense of their employees and their service offerings. Airlines and automobile manufacturers are crying – not serving better or raising quality. They're cutting everything and everyone, and begging for money. Morale is in the gutter, along with service. HUGE mistake.

EASY ANSWER: Double your service offerings.

REALITY: People are looking to get closer, to find a bond, to find answers. People want the country to rally and win. Patriotism is rampant. (What was your last PROACTIVE act of patriotism?) It's not just salute the flag and sing the national anthem. It's look at history and see how we have overcome adversity in the past, and try to discover and work for positive outcomes in the future.

WAKE UP: Now is the time for friendly, and friendly itself is change that makes other change possible. Now is the time for service, and service itself can make people want to do business with you at all times, not just economically challenging times.

YOUR CRISIS: Eventually every leader faces some form of crisis. A downturn. A financial shortage. A fire. A hurricane. A death. An accident. Something gone wrong. When these situations occur, they call for true leadership. With little time to think, hopefully there's a plan because action must be taken immediately. Decisive action.

This is where your true character can shine in a manner that will always be remembered. This is a time when your actions and your commands will always be remembered, regardless of the outcome.

When crisis situations occur, your mental assessment must be instantaneous. This is where your resilience comes in. This is when you remain calm and self-assured, and ready to decide, delegate, and do.

As leader, you must stay in the middle of the fray and help others do their part, still maintaining your leadership position, but clearly willing to be hands-on and involved.

KEY POINT OF UNDERSTANDING: Crisis comes in two forms: I've experienced this before OR this is brand new. The sister of crisis is emergency, usually from something medical, and it requires immediate attention and personal follow up. If you experience something for the first time, consider immediate options and (if possible) find someone to collaborate with to make certain your thinking is clear and grounded before acting. If you have experienced it before, let your resilience kick in and let your known wisdom take over.

KEY ACTION TO TAKE: Have an emergency phone list for everyone and everything that could take place. Make certain that everyone on your team has the list. Be certain the list includes everyone's cell phone number. In times of emergency, instant communication is a key factor in determining outcome.

Change is not a four-letter word... but often your reaction to it is!

— *Jeffrey Gitomer*

Help – We're Growing. Help – the Market is Changing. Help – the Economy is in the Tank. Help – We're Merging. Help – My Budget's Been Slashed. Help – Change!

When big companies make moves, the results are felt by the people that helped make them big, or helped keep them big, or helped them get bigger.

Whether it's the economy, a merger, a "change in comp plan" (also known as reduction in pay), or the introduction of a new product, things change every day in the business world.

I want to address some of the elements of change, acknowledge their reality, and in the process rename the situation to one that is more easily understood by those on the receiving end. You.

Change comes about either by greed, or by taking advantage of opportunity, or by corporate growth, or by evolution to a better way, or by outside economic forces, or from internal economic conditions, or to appease Wall Street (cut costs and increase earnings), or by modernization, or by innovation. And did I mention greed?

Reality bites.

"We had to make some tough decisions" means a hammer is about to fall.

"Today we are announcing the merger of…" means everyone will be in panic mode about their job.

Change brought about by the reasons stated above often brings a lowering of morale inside the company. Especially if management is not communicating well. And low morale leads to lower productivity, lack of service response, and (ultimately) a loss of customers.

There are different ways to look at change.

On the dark side:

- **Change is eliminating.**
- **Change is terminating.**
- **Change is hiding or avoiding truth.**
- **Change is disappointing.**
- **Change is scary.**
- **Change is morale busting.**

On the bright side:

- **Change is refinement.**
- **Change is growth.**
- **Change is movement.**
- **Change is acquiring.**
- **Change is upgrading.**
- **Change is opportunity.**

In order for it to be most effective and have a positive outcome, change must be communicated by leadership in a straightforward way – not *downsize* or *right-size* – it's layoff and job elimination – and then state the REAL reason – not making enough profit – duplication of title in a merger – lack of sales. Unfortunately, this is rarely done.

Here is the reality, the remedy, and a few personal rules as you react to change:

KEEP YOUR ATTITUDE UP: Rather than "this sucks," make a plan for what can be done. Make a plan for what you can do. If nothing can be done, or what can be done falls short of your ideals, make a plan to get out.

KEEP YOUR THOUGHTS FOCUSED ON DOING YOUR BEST: In mergers or slower economic times, companies keep their BEST people. Be your best. Instead of "waiting to see what happens," decide to be your best, ask how you can help, and lead the charge. Set a positive example, and work as hard as you can, so that whatever happens, you will always be able to say you did your best until the last minute of the last day.

KEEP YOUR MIND OPEN TO OTHER POSSIBILITIES: What would you really like to do? Why aren't you doing that anyway?

STAY AWAY FROM (DON'T GET INVOLVED IN) POLITICS AND PITY PARTIES: Odds are that if you're dissatisfied with what is happening, so are others. Stay away from groaners, whiners, and other assorted non-solution oriented people. Waste of your time and energy.

DON'T LOSE FAITH: Your outlook on what could or should happen will determine your willingness to work hard now. Faith in yourself and your circumstance will carry the day. Change happens daily. Don't get nervous – get excited. No matter what happens, the sun will come up tomorrow. Fear of the unknown is always greater than fear of the known. There are no easy answers when you're in the heat of the fire. Follow your heart, and your wallet will catch up.

NOTE WELL: If you have a family, meet with them and get their ideas and their support. Your family wants the best for you. Talk to them. Get closer to the people you love in times of transition.

BIG AHA!: When there is market upheaval, economic uncertainty, or merger, people tend to look inward and ask themselves, "Is my job safe?" and then take the appropriate steps to play internal politics or waste their day(s) making sure all is well. The biggest vulnerability in uncertain times is NOT your job – it's your customers. They are the revenue source that will ultimately provide your job security. Don't guard your job – guard your customers. Serve them memorably. Sell them more. Keep them loyal. And earn referrals from them.

If you want "change insurance" or "change assurance" recognize that it doesn't come from your boss. It comes from your customers. Guard them with your life.

Often you cannot affect the change – it affects you. Your responsibilities in dealing with the changing elements of life and career are to:

- Understand them first (no knee jerk reactions).

- Create the attitude of acceptance.

- View change as a challenge and learning experience.

- Make a plan to harmonize with those things or people that affect you.

- Speak about changes in a supportive way.

- Focus on adaptability – your ability to compromise.

- Act on changes in a building way.

- Maintain your positive attitude at all costs.

- Don't allow change to divert your focus and drive to succeed.

- Adopt the perception that you will take advantage of change.

NEW IS BETTER: We buy "new" in the grocery store. It's the second most powerful marketing word (*free* is first). If people crave it in the store and eat it up on TV, why do they resist it – actually fight it on the job?

Here's why:

- **Fear of the unknown.**
- **Fear of loss of existing security.**
- **Poor attitude toward growth.**
- **Lack of self-confidence that they can adapt.**
- **Lack of desire or personal motivation to change.**

DON'T GET TRAPPED: There are pitfalls to beware of. Others may not be able to take change like you can. Don't get caught up in their crap, er *trap*. Don't join their pity party and don't agree with their plight. Suggest good things or solutions and offer a meeting to discuss and uncover opportunities.

Add one *new inevitable* to the original two. Death and taxes. Change. Harness its power and succeed – fight it and fail.

A leader's ability to accept change – adapt to change, convert change to opportunity, and communicate that opportunity to your team – is at the fulcrum point of their ability to succeed.

Here are 10.5 ways to adapt to and take advantage of change so you can naturally and positively incorporate it into your life – and your life's work:

1. Just accept change as part of life. It's inevitable – don't fight it. Give change a chance.

2. Keep change in perspective. It ain't brain cancer – it's not death. It's something new and different. It might be better.

3. Look for new opportunities to succeed. You'll never see how change can work in your favor if you're mad.

4. Write down all the bad things that could possibly happen. Then figure out a game plan to avert or deal with each one of them.

5. Write down all the good things that can come of change. Then expand on the opportunities they can bring you and your company.

6. Discuss your concerns with others WHO CAN HELP. Avoid those who are grumbling or wallowing in self-pity.

7. Don't "WOE IS ME" it. Seek out others less fortunate than you to keep things in perspective.

8. Form a team to figure out positive outcomes. Explore as much possible good from change as you (and others) are able.

9. Keep your attitude level and reinforcement at an all-time high. Now is the time to listen to and read as much about positive attitude as you can. Keep your car brain full of inspiring words from the masters.

10. Goal three things that will make the change work. List the opportunities that the change provides. Then go on an all-out action plan to achieve those goals.

10.5 Remember that you're the greatest. This change is an opportunity to prove it to yourself and achieve new greatness. Just roll along – just change it.

KEY POINT OF UNDERSTANDING: Although rarely received well at first, organizational change, policy change, and/or people change represents the biggest opportunity for growth and leadership stability. Change is what resilience is all about. Your opportunity to understand, react, respond, and recover in a positive way. NOTE WELL: Opportunities mean nothing unless you take advantage of them.

KEY ACTION TO TAKE: Rather than list goals, list the many opportunities that change has created. When you do, goals have a chance to follow in a positive and more constructive manner. Start by stating what can be done; not what can't be done. For example, if a merger is taking place, the opportunity may be to positively communicate this news to customers or fellow employees. The goal would be to create a short note of information and a request for dialog and ideas.

STRENGTH

9

GUTS
LEADERSHIP

The strength to decide
and delegate, and the strength to
handle any situation or person
that challenges your authority
or ability to lead.

Having the Guts to Decide.

Many leaders take too long to make a decision and, as a result, task productivity and overall achievement are hampered by a degree of frustration. Your job as leader is to decide and move forward.

Yes, decisions must be calculated, based on all risk factors, measured against possible wins and losses, and looked at as to both short-term and long-term value.

Regardless of the process that you go through, long decision cycles are not just unproductive; they also hurt morale. And you, as a leader, are viewed as indecisive.

I'm challenging you that there are very few "safe" decisions. Many people who were safe with the idea of buying IBM came to the realization that they made the wrong decision and eventually competitors came in who were faster and better (not necessarily cheaper) and began to erode IBM's market share.

KEY POINT OF UNDERSTANDING: Making a decision is not just your process, or your risk. It can be collaborative. But it must be swift. Others are waiting, and measuring.

KEY ACTION TO TAKE: Right or wrong – DECIDE QUICKLY.

The Leadership Delta

By: Jeff Holcomb

AUTHOR'S NOTE: Jeff Holcomb is a real leader. Decorated US Army Special Forces/Green Beret, he has experienced life, death, and leadership in a way that most people have only read about. His split-second decisions have saved lives. His loyalty runs so deep it cannot be measured. And he has chosen to continue on his success path by training other leaders. Thousands of them. I have asked Jeff to share some of his philosophies and strategies with you. He is writing his own book that will elaborate on both how he gained his experience and what he learned in the process. Put his book on the TOP of your 2012 "must buy" list.

As we humans climbed out of the primordial ooze, and began our trek from caveman to CEO, our evolution was supercharged primarily because we had sufficient grey matter to ask these two very important age-old questions: *What is it? How do I make it better?*

In keeping with my mammoth-hunting forefathers, I too have endeavored to apply this prehistoric evolutionary refinement process.

My topic of choice is Leadership. So, Leadership. What is it? My military experience would define leadership as "The art and science of providing purpose, direction, and motivation to an individual, team, or group to complete a desired mission, goal, or end-state."

This is a very broad definition and just the three words purpose, direction, and motivation have launched thousands of books and organizational models.

As a young 24-year-old Special Forces commando, I rationalized that to be an effective and successful leader (and not to mention stay alive), I would need to take the given leadership definition, and further apply those same two age-old questions:

What is it?
How do I make it better?

I have continued to apply these two perennial questions in relation to leadership my entire life. Thank goodness for sages like Ram Charan, Paul Hersey, Jack Welch, and many other military and business leadership visionaries to help light my way.

One of my key leaders (and a mentor) was General Pete Schoomaker. I first met him when he was the US Army's Delta Force Commander. His "Coyote's Rules" established the left and right limits of the global grey playing field on which we would operate.

Following his example, I created my own set of principles to assist my team as I delegated responsibility (sometimes life-and-death responsibility).

It is interesting to note, with the exception of a few words, these principles have not changed as I have transitioned into civilian business leadership roles.

Here are Pancho's 7 Principles (my radio call-sign while in Green Berets was Pancho):

1. Integrity is my foundation. Never consider or accept anything that is illegal, immoral, or unethical.

2. My customers and employees are my life-blood. Without them I (and my team) do not have a real good reason to exist. We are each servant leaders that provide clear purpose, direction, and motivation.

3. When in charge, I take charge. "Lead and be decisive" is not AN option, it's the ONLY option. An army of sheep led by lions will defeat an army of lions led by sheep.

4. Achieve excellence through strong, positive, collaborative communication. A challenge is not an excuse to stop. It is an opportunity to create new and stronger relationships, and it's an opportunity to achieve and win as a group.

5. I am proactive at every turn. A reactive mindset will exhaust you. When possible, have a PACE (Primary, Alternate, Contingency, Emergency) plan.

6. Maintain technological relevancy. My technology moves literally at light speed, and so does yours. Social media, predictive analytics, and lines of mobile, verbal, and written communication are evolving daily. Stay relevant or retire!

7. Always help people win. Beyond win-win, I have learned that by helping the other guy think he wins, I win. Be gracious (except on the battlefield) and be positive (on every field, and with every person).

One's ability to read a situation, and to also assess those individuals involved within that situation, is a life or death skill when applied in the Military Special Operations continuum. It was my exposure and training in these perceptive skills as a young Special Operator that cultivated a lifelong obsession with understanding the leadership micro and macro world around me.

Specifically, why if given two individuals, departments, or enterprises with similar education, beliefs, behavior, and skill would one be successful and the other flounder? And, was it possible for me as a leader to intercede and create an opportunity for the floundering entity to move into the ranks of the successful? My personal hypothesis is a model that is exceptionally simple in theory, but profound in application. I call it The *Leadership Delta*.

It defines and challenges at the same time. The Leadership Delta asks you to self assess your ability to utilize specific and task-related data combined with existing skills to Self Diagnose, challenges your courage and fortitude to Self Start, and demands your intelligence to Self Correct as you progress through the task or assignment. It then provides you the systems to immediately move back into Self Diagnose as a constant way to achieve, and as a learning continuum.

In my experience, The Leadership Delta will differentiate the successful from those who flounder, or worse fail to even try. It doesn't force you to be a leader, it challenges you to *use your best leadership skills and talent to their highest degree available*, and *learn more to improve the next time*. In essence, it puts you in charge of you.

Think of the people you know that had a great idea, but never moved on it – or entrepreneurs that knew the challenge blocking their success, but were unable to overcome it – or those who were unable to adapt to the customer or the market, and went under.

All of them, as diverse as they are, are missed opportunities (maybe even once-in-a-lifetime opportunities). That's where The Leadership Delta model plays a vital role.

The Leadership Delta is very simple in theory. It ensures constant self-evaluation, continued education, and drives personal/organizational, technological, and operational relevancy. The model reveals introspective purpose and can be applied at the individual contributor level, leader of others level, leader of leaders level, functional leader, and business or enterprise leader levels.

My lifelong passion is servant leadership. In my opinion, one could spend an entire life focused on just this discipline, and it would be a life well spent. I have been blessed to have many great military and civilian leaders appear at exactly the time when I most needed them. It is their examples and lessons that I have endeavored to assimilate, emulate, and communicate. It is the depth and profound impact of the theory, doctrine, development, discipline, training, application, and execution of leadership that drives me to continue to ask the ever refining questions: *What is it? And how do I make it better?*

Free Git✗Bit...For Jeff Holcomb's bio and contact information, go to www.gitomer.com and enter the word GREEN BERET in the GitBit box.

The Reality of a Wild Card.

Often referred to as a joker, in my experience I have found that one out of every 25 people on any team is a wild card. A wild card would be defined as someone who would rather do it their own way, someone who does not want to follow the authority given, a rule bender (if not a rule breaker) – but someone who has great talent.

Your responsibility as a leader is to harness that individual's power so that he or she is able to work in harmony with the others.

A wild card may require extra coaching; a wild card may also take the assignment of specialized tasks. It may even mean that the wild card will work alone or only with those they get along with.

But as wild as they may be, his or her results are more often than not well worth the extra effort that it takes to make them a productive team member.

KEY POINT OF UNDERSTANDING: To simply say that everyone is different is too simplistic of a statement. Rather, I would say that everyone has a different trigger, everyone has a different motivator, and everyone has a different key reason why he or she wants to be involved and why he or she wants to perform. As leader, your job is to know all and delegate tasks and projects accordingly. The more you focus on strengths and personally motivated desires, the more you will reap the productivity that you seek.

KEY ACTION TO TAKE: Select one wild card on your team. Schedule an hour, maybe a casual breakfast or lunch, and try to dig deeper into their personal motivation – to discover what challenges them and what frustrates them. This will give you insight that will help you delegate to their strength and result in productivity.

Pain in the Ass People.

I ask audiences of sales leaders and business owners, "How many of you have pain in the ass salespeople?"

Everyone raises a hand. Would you?

There are two kinds of pain in the ass people:

1. They're a pain in the ass to everyone in the company. Always grumbling, always complaining, always breaking the rules, and always in some form of trouble or at least an accident waiting to happen. Fire those people as soon as you can. I don't care how good they are. I don't care how important they are to you. They're ruining the morale of your entire company and their replacement will always be better.

2. They're only a pain in the ass to you. That would be your problem. Set meetings with the person and begin to build a better relationship. Get more personal about why they're working for the company and what you can do to help them achieve their business goals not just their personal goals.

Often the most disruptive people are the most productive. They need more attention, they need more help, and they need more coaching.

9

Invest time in your best people and harness their power.

The other side of disruption is a productivity decrease of other people (because of gossip and complaining), and pain in the ass people go against the grain, causing morale and attitude problems. They create real leadership challenges that must be met head-on.

KEY POINT OF UNDERSTANDING: There will always be pain in the ass people. Your job is to be so close to the day-to-day that the person becomes evident to you early on so that you can take action, and be close enough to your key people so that they might act as police, and keep you informed. As a leader, you can't let a personality conflict get in the way of productivity or achievement. You hold the position of authority and can't let personal prejudice get in the way of success.

KEY ACTION TO TAKE: Identify the person vital to the group, but who remains a thorn under your saddle. Reach out and meet with them. Find their passion and identify their barriers. Help them achieve. Be certain that you also reach out to the people they are affecting, and let them know you're aware of the situation and are handling it.

The Delegation.

Most of the leaders I know believe that they are the only person to handle a given situation, a given project, or a given task. As a result, their leadership ability suffers. I've seen this at the highest level of Corporate America.

It's interesting that those same people complain about their workload and their inability to get things done on time, or at least in a timely manner.

There's a key question to ask yourself each time one of these situations arises. It's a two-word question: Who else?

Over the past two years, I have given away more and more of my responsibilities so that I can have more opportunity to concentrate on my best abilities and better task myself with the things that I really love to do – writing being one of them.

At this very moment, my business is running and the people running it are doing the best they can. Sure, they need my help from time to time. Sure, they need my input from time to time. But I'm not the one doing the work. I've delegated leadership authority to others who are acting on my behalf and doing their best (or should I say, being the best Jeffrey they possibly can be).

Yes, mistakes will happen. Yes, errors will be made. But business is running.

In 1976, I visited a company in Brooklyn, New York, called Brooklyn Handkerchief. They were manufacturers of scarves and other printable materials that were integral to the textile screen-printing industry I was involved in.

Meeting with the owners, we engaged in the production and productivity of their product and how to bring it to market.

As I toured their facility, I couldn't help but notice all the things they could be doing better. (That's a nice way of saying "things that they were doing wrong.")

Their president, a wise old man named Milton Cade, looked me in the eye and said, "Jeffrey, sometimes chips fall on the ground. You cannot pick up every chip. Often it's better just to leave them to lay there."

Interesting wisdom that I've never forgotten. I know I'm the best person to do every task in my company, but often I'll give it to the second best person, and lose a few chips. And so must you.

KEY POINT OF UNDERSTANDING: Look at your workload. Focus only on the tasks and people that leap forward. Forget about the minutia – especially the drama of "who struck John."

KEY ACTION TO TAKE: Let go of the unimportant. Delegate with full instructions. Delegate with full empowerment. Delegate with total encouragement. Delegate as much as you can. Measure it and move on.

To Hire or Not to Hire.

I have a two-word hiring philosophy: HIRE EAGLES.

I try to hire the most capable people I can find – never for a moment thinking that they might be better than I am, much less threaten my job. Eagles are people who are strong, fly high, work well alone, take care of each other – and they eat rats.

In today's world, hiring often involves HR Departments who give CYA Tests to individuals in order to determine their suitability to the job. Personally, I do not believe in the validity of those tests.

Here's the criteria you should look at when hiring someone to fill any position in your company: Smart, happy, self-starting, honest, reliable, stays until the job is done, past history of success, and a hunger to succeed. Someone who wants to learn as much as they want to earn. Someone who has a passion for the tasks that they will be performing. And someone with a service heart that can take achievement with personal pride – but someone who expresses that pride as gratitude, rather than bragging.

Those are qualities that do not appear on any test.

Yes, in these times background checks are important. Yes, in these times references need to be checked to corroborate resume facts.

> But the one thing missing from any test or any background check is your gut feeling. Guts have been replaced by tests – and I challenge you to reverse that trend.

Following your gut feeling, your instinct, will not only give you a better person, but it will also challenge you to take your knowledge of people to a new and better level.

KEY POINT OF UNDERSTANDING: You're hiring a person, not a test result. You're going to be relying on and depending on this person to achieve in your environment under your direction. With that responsibility, you have to have a good feeling about who you're hiring. And that feeling comes from within.

KEY ACTION TO TAKE: Whenever I was considering a salesperson to hire or not to hire, I would discount all their references from past employers or teachers and ask them for the name of three customers that they've had dealings with. Those customers would reveal every characteristic of that salesperson, good and bad. In the end, the salesperson has to deal with customers to be successful. Whoever you're talking to has to have dealings with people on their job. If it's a purchasing agent, they've had dealings with vendors. If it's an accountant, they've had dealings with CPA firms. As you consider people for employment, it's most important that you know who he or she has dealt with and what that experience was. That answer will not be A, B, C, or D. That answer will be black and white. Clear as day.

To Fire or Not to Fire.

Some people, based on their attitude, their capability, their productivity, or their ability to get along with others, just need to be successful someplace else.

Your job as a leader is to terminate them quickly, legally, and with their dignity intact.

I've had the displeasure of firing many people in my 40-year career. None of those firings took more than 15 minutes. The longer you talk, the more reasons you'll have to give and the more you will hurt the person who is leaving.

Tell the person you don't believe the fit is right between he/she and your company, and that today is the day you should part ways. Tell the person what the detail is – how much severance, how much insurance, and how much vacation pay – and have all documents prepared. Thank them. Tell them if you're willing to provide a reference or not. Wish them luck. Ask them for all their belongings of yours (keys, passwords, whatever).

Escort them to their desk to gather their personal things. And escort them out the door. Immediately have their e-mail forwarded to someone else in a managerial capacity and have all of their internal passwords and codes changed.

If they have a company cell phone, make them turn it in. And if they have a company computer, make sure it is turned in immediately.

If they have a non-compete clause, be benevolent.
(Non-compete clauses are being struck down all over
the country, and as a businessperson you're seen as evil
for forbidding someone to work elsewhere in the field
they are an expert in order to provide for their family.)

After the initial emotion of being fired or let go wears off, you want the person to be able to say that you were fair to them and that you let them keep their dignity. And maybe after a few years he or she will say, "best boss I ever had."

REALITY: Sometimes firing is ugly, and the aftermath can
be even uglier. The strategy I've given you above is how to
keep an uncomfortable situation as pretty as possible, and
as comfortable as possible.

IMPORTANT NOTE: Do not delegate firing – unless you're
grooming a new leader. If you're firing someone from
the opposite sex, make sure more than two people are
in the room.

And whatever you do, especially in a large corporation, have everything you are about to do well documented in advance so that there's "just cause" in the event of a dispute.

Firing is tough. Leaders have to be tougher.

PC NOTE: The word "firing" is probably better known in HR circles as "terminated." I think you get the meaning. I grew up in an era of different words. Homeless people were called bums. Words have changed. No one is a secretary anymore – or a stewardess, or a waitress. I may be "old word" but I am not "old world."

I fight it. Several years ago I attended a Unitarian church service, and the minister proudly proclaimed that they had completely removed gender from the songbook. I yelled out spontaneously, "Yeah, but they still call it a hymn." Couldn't help it.

KEY POINT OF UNDERSTANDING: No one wants to be fired. And no one wants to fire. Both people in the room are uncomfortable in the room once the cat is out of the bag. Oftentimes people know that they're going to be fired, are waiting for the hammer to drop, and are actually relieved that the act has finally taken place. As a leader, you will also be relieved when you have done a clean job of it. You may not be doing the best for the person involved. But you are going to be doing the best for your company.

KEY ACTION TO TAKE: Have every document, every number, every detail, and every dollar accounted for prior to the firing meeting so that any question that is asked by the person being fired can clearly and immediately be responded to.

STRENGTH

10

PERSONAL LEADERSHIP

The strength to re-dedicate
yourself to self-education and
personal excellence as your
leadership tenure matures.

Can Leaders Influence Without Authority? … Hardly.

I just read this quote: "The key to successful leadership today is influence, not authority." WHAT? Eh, not quite.

It's sounds good when you first hear it, but it's not only completely without merit, it's also downright dangerous.

The quote should say, "One of the MANY keys to successful leadership today is influence." It bugs me when someone attempts wisdom, and it flies in the face of logic, emotion, and especially reality.

If you think a leader can lead with no authority to lead, re-think that immediately. Imagine a person of great influence standing outside a major corporation, but not having a job at the company, let alone a position of authority. Would anyone take action? Would anyone follow that guy? Would anyone even listen?

The "influencer with no authority" would probably get his biggest chance telling it to the judge after being hauled off by security.

Same in government. Can you imagine a person of influence trying to lead, manage, or vote on an issue with no authority? Not gonna EVER happen.

REALITY: There is no "key" to successful leadership. Short quotes like that are not only misinforming, they're downright dangerous, unless you are already a leader, and already have authority. The authority to influence.

REALITY: There is no one key to leadership. You need a fat set of keys that includes BOTH authority and influence. And anyone who tells you differently is trying to exert their influence, without an ounce of authority.

Here are the elements, totally based on authority, that give real leaders the ability to influence:

- **Respect.** If respect for the leader is lost, the power of influence AND authority are weak at the foundation of any mission. Leaders make the mistake of commanding respect when, in fact, respect is earned.

- **Clarity of message.** If leaders are to be followed, it starts with clarity of message.

- **Positive attitude that sets an example for others to adopt.** Attitude is THE fundamental element that creates a path for all leaders to succeed, not just influence.

- **Ability to motivate.** Creating the desire of the team to perform at top level. Real leaders create that drive for the person first, the mission second, and the leader last.

- **Ability to inspire.** The difference between motivation and inspiration is that motivation must constantly be injected. Inspiration lasts a lifetime. Great leaders can instill both.

- **Ability to strategize.** Well-founded strategies are eagerly accepted by your team. They make sense and they seem doable.

- **Ability to plan, and plan B.** After strategy is decided, plans (and alternate plans) are drawn to achieve the strategy. Plan B is also created to assure no loss of forward momentum in case there's an unexpected shift or change.

- **Resilience.** One of the least understood, and possibly the element that carries the most "success weight" is resilience. A leader's ability to take it, and give it back, or bounce back from whatever situation arises. An influential leader with low or no resilience will not be in that position very long.

- **Past experience.** A history of both success and failure that has provided the knowledge and wisdom to lead in the present.

- **Persuasion.** A higher form of influence. Persuasion occurs when trust and confidence meet belief, risk tolerance, and safety.

- **Stature.** Leaders must stand tall and be recognized for their posture, confidence, and poise.

- **Character.** The elements that build the profile. Character is possessed (or lost) by consistently "doing the right and the best thing." Character plays a major role in a leader's ability to influence. Great character is molded over time.

- **Image.** Actions, results, and reputation combine to form image.

- **Ethics.** This element of leadership determines reputation. Great leaders operate at and with the highest ethical standards.

- **By example.** As a business leader, business person, and entrepreneur myself for more than 40 years, I have ALWAYS set the example by "doing" rather than "telling" or "demanding." Don't tell me what to do. Show me how it's done.

- **Tolerance of risk.** Great leaders have a high risk tolerance, and a sense to know when to take a calculated one.

- **Ability to get along with others.** I believe that "likeability" plays a major role in a leader's ability to create productivity and achievement.

- **Courage.** The intestinal fortitude to withstand all adversity, and the resilience to react, respond, and recover on the way to accomplishment, achievement, and victory.

- **Ability to achieve.** Great leaders are not just respected; they're also measured. They have the responsibility to achieve, and their effectiveness is measured against their charged tasks and goals.

- **Ability to withstand failure.** A major part of resilience, failure must serve as a lesson, and an opportunity to grow. Sure, there is disappointment, sometimes anger – but leadership does not rest on a single event. All great leaders have encountered, withstood, endured, and recovered from defeat – much wiser, and much more steadfast of purpose.

- **Ability to celebrate victory.** Everyone wants to celebrate a victory. Real leaders know how to create genuine celebration AND recognition of all those who participated. They also know how to temper it, and use it as a springboard for the next task at hand.

- **Reputation.** Everything discussed above creates and forms a leader's reputation. Reputation creates the ability to attract and the desire for others to follow. And reputation often arrives on the scene way before the leader does. Not just a "great guy" or a "take charge" person, rather someone "known" as a great leader and has earned the respect of his/her people and his/her community.

Including authority and the ability to influence, I have just given you 22 vital characteristics of leadership and the ability to lead. No single characteristic holds the magic. But together they are the keys to become a dominant leader when each of them is mastered.

Free GitBit... If you want more leadership growth information go to www.gitomer.com and enter the words GROW MANAGER in the GitBit box.

What REALLY Motivates?

- Money
- Encouragement
- Opportunity
- Fear
- Family
- Achievement
- Independence
- Challenge
- Love of job
- Belief in product
- Recognition
- Desire to win
- Desire to succeed

What REALLY Inspires?

My partner Jessica and I have spent the last 24 months attending as many musical concerts and events as time will allow us to.

Panic! at the Disco, Gladys Knight, Justin Timberlake, Kanye West, Rihanna, Bruce Springsteen, Maroon 5, Stevie Wonder, The Police, Smokey Robinson, Les Paul, Elvis Costello, "LOVE" (a Cirque du Soleil Beatles tribute), "Jersey Boys," Tony Bennett, a '50s doo-wop revival, The Cure.

Last week we witnessed the great Leonard Cohen.

Of course the recent event is the most prominent, but for more reasons than one. Leonard Cohen is an original. My first exposure was in the 1960s. He is influential both as a poet and a songwriter-performer.

Cohen's concert made my emotional cup run over. For 3.5 hours, I screamed, sang along, clapped, cheered, lit a match (I shined my iPhone), laughed, and cried. At 75 years young, he and his musically impeccable band evoked cheers, tears, wild applause, three encores, and made a timeless musical statement that stamped my mind and heart.

These concerts have helped my attitude and my sales. They have given me an emotional and inspirational charge. And if you want the definition of diversity, re-read the list.

Music makes all my emotions deeper and all my thoughts sharper. And not just in concert – also before sales calls and appointments. I play upbeat music on my way to give a presentation. I inspire myself. I set my own soul on fire. And I walk into the prospect's office rocking, and feeling great about the meeting.

How about you? If you love music, why not incorporate more of it into your business life?

Music makes a memory. If I play the right song I can take you back to an exact place in time. First date, first kiss, first husband, first wife, summer vacation, high school, college, affairs of the heart – the list of memories through song is endless.

Here's a simple exercise: List your current five favorite songs. Now list five favorites from your past. Next to each song, put down what it means to you. The current songs probably won't mean much other than you like them and listen to them often. The ones from the past are another story. They will present you with times, places, people, and clear memories.

PERSONAL SECRET: I learned my presentation skills singing karaoke in bars.

If you doubt the power of music, consider these facts:

- **Music inspires your thoughts and thinking.**

- **Music affirms your memories and truths.**

- **Music helps you smile and recall pleasant experiences.**

- **Listening and singing sets an internal musical mood.**

- **Music reinforces your internal positive attitude.**

- **Music creates a feeling of rhythm.**

- **Music creates an emotional surge that enters your mind and soul when you hear certain songs.**

- **Music is transferable and transformational.**

- **Music is familiar. Even if you can't sing a note, when you're alone in the car you're singing along.**

- **Music is mystical and it makes you feel good.**

KEY POINT OF UNDERSTANDING: Music soothes the soul, lifts the spirit, inspires action, and fills the wallet.

KEY ACTION TO TAKE: List your current five favorite songs. Now list five favorites from your past. Next to each song, put down what it means to you. The current songs probably won't mean much other than you like them and listen to them often. The ones from the past are another story. They will present you with times, places, people, and clear memories. Go out and find your music. Listening and singing will give you mental, physical, and monetary rewards.

Win One for the Gipper? Eh, Not This Year.

Knute Rockne was one of the greatest coaches of all time. Innovative, fiery, emotional, a great speaker, a winner who coached some of the greatest football players of all time. The four horsemen, George Gipp, Frank Leahy, and Curly Lambeau. Rockne won several national championships, and he put Notre Dame on the football map forever.

He was a strong leader of men.

Rockne popularized the forward pass, created the shift offense, and took every risk possible to win. That was then. This is now.

I'm certain you've seen or heard of the movie *Knute Rockne, All American* in which Rockne (played by Pat O'Brien) encourages his team to "Win one for the Gipper!"

George Gipp (played by Ronald Reagan), one of the greatest and most versatile athletes of all time (quarterback, running back, defensive back, punter, punt and kickoff returner – all in the same game – for four seasons), died tragically in 1920 during his senior season of a throat infection.

The legend goes that Rockne was at Gipp's bedside just before he died. His last words were, "I've got to go, Rock. It's all right. I'm not afraid. Some time, Rock, when the team is up against it, when things are wrong and the breaks are beating the boys, ask them to go in there with all they've got, and win just one for the Gipper. I don't know where I'll be then, Rock. But I'll know about it, and I'll be happy."

Rockne used the emotion of Gipp's death to deliver one of the greatest locker room talks of all time. At halftime he used the story of Gipp, along with his deathbed wish, to inspire Notre Dame to an underdog, come-from-behind victory at Yankee Stadium over the undefeated Army team of 1928.

Knute Rockne, All American – great movie. But, it's a *movie*, not real life. And society has changed a bit since 1920 (or 1940 when the movie was made).

People want to win for themselves – NOT THE GIPPER.

As leader, you must encourage your people to produce, win, and succeed – BUT to do it for their right reasons – mortgage payments, car payments, tuition, vacations.

We as a people, we as a country, have narrowed down the options of what and who we're willing to "win one" for. Win one for America and defeat the enemy for freedom? Hell yes! Win one for the company, the sales manager, the boss? Hell no!

"WIN ONE" REALITY: Your people want to win for themselves, their kids, their mortgage payment, their new car, their kid's tuition, their vacation. Not you.

HERE'S THE SECRET: Help them win for their reasons, and they'll help you win for yours.

To Serve is to Rule.

The most powerful people I know are givers. The most selfish people I know are takers. (Also described by Ayn Rand in *Atlas Shrugged* as "looters" or "moochers" and described by General George Patton as "people pulling against you.")

There are three qualities I believe to be at the core of a leader's greatness and legacy:

- **A service heart.**

- **Genuine humility.**

- **Eternal gratefulness.**

These three qualities, when blended, create an opportunity for you to dominate your position in a benevolent way.

Others will serve you because they know that you serve them. Others will be grateful to you because they know that you are grateful to them and for them. Others will respect you because your humility is perceived as part of your fabric.

CAUTION: It's never everybody. There will be people on your team who envy you, who you have become, who you are, and where you're headed. Some will even speak ill of you. The best thing (and the hardest thing) to do is ignore them. If you're able to turn a deaf ear and watch them waving about, maybe you can picture them as cheerleaders.

Not everyone will appreciate you. Not everyone will take you the right way. Not everyone will be happy with the actions that you take. But if you're genuine about why you're taking them (not to serve yourself but rather to serve others), and if your sincerity is evident, then you can keep your peace of mind that you're doing your best for everyone, including yourself.

In my writings I have used the expression, "People will rain on your parade, because they have no parade of their own." It's especially true as it relates to your attitude and your acceptance that not all good comes from good intentions.

KEY POINT OF UNDERSTANDING: When looking to serve, it's not who they are, it's who you are. "Serve your best and love the rest," is the best way to look at the people you lead. Don't just be grateful for your opportunities and your people. Be more grateful for who you are and what you have to offer.

KEY ACTION TO TAKE: Record some of your conversations and listen to them. Record your presentations and listen to them. Record your meetings and listen to them. One listen will tell you about your service, your humility, and your gratefulness. Resolve to do better and be better and make a 12-month plan to record, listen, and improve.

If they **LIKE** you, and they believe you, and they have confidence in you, and they trust you, and they respect you – they will be loyal to you and they will follow you. It starts with **LIKE**.

– Jeffrey Gitomer

A Few More Personal Leadership Insights…

Transferability. You may have tremendous knowledge and tremendous experience, and you may have answers that will work and win for almost every situation that arises, but if your ability to transfer that message is weak, then the outcomes you're hoping for will fall short of the mark. The keys to your ability to successfully transfer your wisdom and your knowledge are personal belief, personal passion, personal enthusiasm, and an ability to present what others perceive as both understandable and sincere.

Acceptability. Why do some ideas work and others fail? Why do some projects get completed while others are abandoned? Why are some delegations carried out perfectly and others wallow in time delay?

I've gone on in depth about leadership concepts and processes throughout the course of this book, only mentioning the one word that I believe defines acceptability once. The word is "fit." If the person you're influencing or trying to influence does not feel that there's a mental or physical "fit" to what you're communicating or delegating, they will fall mentally short of desire to complete. There has to be both a comfort level and a belief of the recipient that they can achieve your tasks or your goals. When that belief is present, then his or her intention to carry out the delegation will be successful.

Transferability and acceptability are significant, yet often misunderstood among leaders. It is your personal responsibility to make each of these elements real in the mind of your people in order for your expected outcomes to be achieved.

– Jeffrey Gitomer

STRENGTH

11

CELEBRATION LEADERSHIP

The strength to recognize,
reward, and celebrate
performance, achievement,
and victory.

Recognize Employee Recognition for What It Is: GOLD!

At the corporate sales meetings where I give presentations, I am often asked to participate in giving out sales awards.

The customer is elated when I say okay. Little do they know it's one of my favorite things to do – and one of, if not THE most important parts of their event.

PLEASE NOTE: These are not "contest" awards. They are sales achievement awards.

People's names are called for one achievement or another and their name and photo are shown on big screens in front of everyone (especially their peers). They walk to the stage to accept their award – smiling, beaming, and full of pride.

Statues are given, plaques are awarded, inscriptions are read aloud, hands are shaken, photos are taken, and prizes are given to the people who won – nay, EARNED the award. All their hard work is recognized and rewarded. In public.

What's the value of this type of ceremony? Can't be measured. (Or to quote MasterCard, "Priceless.")

You can measure performance, but you can't measure pride of achievement. Nor can you measure the motivation and inspiration to continue to achieve.

Their stimulus is not measured in some government handout or bailout. It's internal stimulus created from personal pride and accomplishment. Winning. Selling.

When someone wins an award there are several unspoken benefits. There is the incentive for that person to maintain or improve his or her performance to stay at the top. And there is HUGE stimulus for others in the audience to try to win an award next year.

Here are the benefits of recognition, rewards, and praise:

- **Recognize salespeople for a job well done, and they will recognize you.**

- **Praise salespeople for a job well done, and they will praise you.**

- **Reward salespeople for a job well done, and they will continue to reward you.**

- **Recognize people for a job well done, and they will recognize you.**

- **Praise people for a job well done, and they will praise you.**

- **Reward people for a job well done, and they will continue to reward you.**

Why don't you take a look at your company, your employees, your salespeople, and your awards and rewards? Maybe some recognition re-org is in order. Maybe instead of "cutting," you might try "investing." Especially in salespeople. They are your bailout.

NOTE: Instead of figuring out how to change (reduce) compensation plans as a disincentive and morale breaker to all, why not invest in a sales meeting and a celebration to reward those who have achieved at the highest level, and challenge those in the audience that they too can win these awards next year if they decide to dedicate the time and effort to do so.

KEY POINT OF UNDERSTANDING: Incentives and awards are economic stimuli of the first degree. Real stimulus. In challenging economic times (how's that for putting it mildly), sales are what will make a company recover. Oh, you may have to make some cuts for the safety of your business, but no company ever cut their way to success. You must sell your way to profit and success.

KEY ACTION TO TAKE: Award achievement in public. Not just in front of your own people – make sure it's on your company's blog, in your weekly e-mail magazine, and posted on your website.

Free GitBit... Want a game plan and list of suggestions for creating incentives and awards for your people? Go to www.gitomer.com and enter the word AWARDS in the GitBit box.

Celebration!

Think back to your youth – when you won a ball game, or your favorite team won a championship. Maybe you played competitive sports and won a race or a match. What was the celebration like? How long did it last? What was your feeling as a result of the win?

That's the kind of celebration that needs to be shared with your people each time a major achievement occurs. Let each person feel that his or her performance is appreciated, and allow the celebrants to have the time and space in which the essence of their victory can sink in.

REALITY: A salesman runs into his boss's office screaming, "I just made a big sale! I just made a big sale!" The boss peeks his head up from the desk and says, "You still have three more to go to make your quota this month." While that scenario sounds pretty bad, if you and I each had a dollar for every time that occurs, we would be millionaires. Each of us.

Ring the bell. Give applause. Give a bonus. Give praise. And create incentive for the next three sales to be made.

Think of Coach Vince Lombardi being carried off the field by his players. It was the players who won the game, but they loved their leader so much that they made him the hero! Who's carrying you off the field?

STRENGTH

12

NEXT-LEVEL LEADERSHIP

The strength to see what's next, accept the challenge, take on the responsibility, and climb the associated ladder.

Leadership 360.5 and 365 – Adding Impact and Measurement to the Standard 360 Process.

AUTHOR'S NOTE: I'm readdressing the 360 assessment process here because I believe it to be so important, yet at the same time so misused or underutilized.

If I asked you if you're a 360 leader, would you answer with more than a shoulder shrug? Have you ever taken a 360 leadership assessment? Why? That assessment is all about you! 360 involves your people, your customers, your vendors, and the way they feel about your ability to lead and serve based on your words, actions, and deeds.

Buzzwords, buzz phrases, and buzz crazes bug me. They never last. If they did, TQM would still be taught instead of being laughed at. And in my opinion, 360 will go the same way.

Words change as times change, but the old words are the true meaning. Waitress, stewardess, and secretary to name a few. To me, 360 is a new word for the old word "feedback." Maybe I'm nuts, but 360 doesn't require a book about it, just a form or a meeting will do. Face-to-face preferably.

And missing from everything I've read on 360 is structure and responsibility for putting that feedback into action, especially as relates to the quality and skills of the leader.

I'm going to call it Leadership 360.5 – *taking action on feedback, especially on a personal level*.

And then there's my other challenge to the 360 concept. Mine is Leadership 365. Leadership opportunities occur every minute of every day (365 days a year) – the questions are *how ready (prepared) are you, how willing (great attitude) are you*, and *how able (past experience and training) are you to take* "resilient *advantage*" *of them?*

Leadership 360 is obvious – how it's executed to the level of "successful outcome desired" is not so obvious.

The missing ingredient is training, or should I say a willingness on the part of the leader to learn what's new and create a continuous improvement learning schedule for him or herself.

KEY POINT OF UNDERSTANDING: 360, 360.5, or 365 – which is it? Answer – it's all three. Or you could just say, give feedback, take feedback, and put all positive constructive feedback into action.

KEY ACTION TO TAKE: Admit you may need to change, or learn (or both) to make both halves of 360 work for yourself and the other 180.

The Lost Secret of Leadership.

If you're looking for some magic formula – some wisdom of the ages – some quote from someone that ties it all together, that's not the secret.

The lost secret of leadership is found in one word: *Encouragement.*

Encouragement is THE key to high self-esteem, high self-image, high attitude, higher productivity, and highest achievement.

Every time someone is seeking to complete a task, complete a project, come close to a milestone, or compete for a victory, your encouragement may be the very words that put him or her over the top.

As a leader, you have the power to influence, and you make a choice to either influence negatively or positively.

The same way you encouraged your one-year-old to walk is the same way you need to encourage your people to succeed, to achieve, and to win.

There's a deeper secret inside the secret: Once you have encouraged, and once that encouragement has resulted in some form of victory – *celebrate it!*

When your one-year-old took their first step, did you celebrate? If they weren't walking fast enough or early enough, did you threaten them with no allowance or no college if they weren't walking within two weeks? Or did you continue to encourage – continue to cheer them on until they finally took those first steps – and then celebrate with hugs, kisses, photographs, and phone calls to anyone or everyone who would listen?

KEY POINT OF UNDERSTANDING: Every poor performance is an opportunity for encouragement. Every great performance is an opportunity to reward and celebrate.

KEY ACTION TO TAKE: Take every member of your team aside this week. Talk to them about what's happening in their day to day. Support them with an idea. Pat them on the shoulder and tell them they're doing a great job. Encourage them to keep hard at it. Tell them you support them and to please let you know if they need anything.

The way you would encourage a one-year-old to walk is the same way you need to encourage your people to succeed, to achieve, and to win.

– Jeffrey Gitomer

Got a Mission? Or Just a Mission Statement?

Is your mission statement really a mission? Or is it a bunch of marketing, mumbo-jumbo BS about how you're gonna dominate the world, exceed expectations, and build shareholder value?

Pardon me while I vomit.

Take a look at any corporate mission statement or vision statement. They're all full of it. They all say nothing. They all mean nothing. Oh, don't get me wrong. Some of them have high ideals, but the problem is there's no implementation plan that accompanies them. No CEO reads the mission statement and says, "Okay everyone, here's my game plan and your action plan for how we're going to implement this."

HERE'S THE REASON: The narrow-minded marketing department or advertising agency that created the mission statement is not capable of creating an implementation plan.

If you're going to be the number one company, *tell me HOW you're going to be the number one company*. If you're going to exceed customer expectations, *tell me HOW you're going to exceed customer expectations*. If you're going to build shareholder value, *tell me HOW you're going to build shareholder value*.

Then give me an implementation plan so that each and every person in the company understands the vision, can take action on the vision, can become proficient at the vision, and can master the vision.

Otherwise, it's just a piece of paper that hangs on a wall.

It never ceases to amaze me how many people in a corporate environment cannot recite their own company's mission statement. They see it posted in the office and it's on their company literature, but not one person can recite it word for word.

Hey, Sparky, It's the mission! It's what you're supposed to march to.

It's the mission! And if the people that created it have no implementation plan for it, then why should anyone bother with it?

KEY POINT OF UNDERSTANDING: Mission statements can create loyalty, both from customers and employees if, *and only if*, there's a plan to implement the mission.

KEY ACTION TO TAKE: Test the validity of YOUR mission. Bring 20 people into your office and ask them to recite the mission. JOKE. Now call your marketing people. Have them visit your top customers and talk to them at the USE OF YOUR PRODUCT OR SERVICE level, where they can find out what really matters. Then tell marketing to create a real mission statement or they're fired. And if it's your ad agency preparing it, save yourself a bunch of time. Just fire them summarily, and WRITE IT YOURSELF.

The Garcia Principle of Mission.

Free Git✗Bit... If you've never read "Message to Garcia," now would be a great time! Go to www.gitomer.com and enter the word GARCIA in the GitBit box. Now.

Written by Elbert Hubbard in 1899, it's about completing a mission. An army officer named Rowan was asked by the president of the United States to "Deliver this message to Garcia." And he did.

On the surface, no big deal. Mission accomplished. The reason this essay has been a classic for more than 100 years are the circumstances and the actions that surround the achievement. And the more we, as a society, try to exercise a whiny pushback, the more relevant "Message to Garcia" becomes.

Rowan accepted the mission without a question. Questions that YOU or your people might ask are: "Who's Garcia? Where does he live? How long is this gonna take? Am I being paid to do this? Will I be back in time to get my kids from daycare?"

Rowan didn't ask any of those self-serving questions. HE JUST DELIVERED THE MESSAGE.

How's your mission? What's your mission? How is it being delivered? Who is delivering it?

Implementing the 1899 "Garcia" principle requires a clearer understanding. Your mission statement should end with the words NO MATTER WHAT. Those words indicate completion, and an understanding of what people are willing to do to make it happen. And it indicates dedication to a successful outcome.

BEHIND the simple message of Message to Garcia are these tough questions:

- **Who's your Garcia?**

- **Who can you rely on?**

- **Who can you depend on?**

- **Who, if you gave them something to do, would you take EVERY CENT out of the bank and bet that they would complete the task?**

- **How reliable are you?**

- **Do your actions match your reputation?**

"Civilization is one long anxious search for just such individuals. Nothing such a man asks shall not be granted. He is wanted in every city, town and village, in every office, shop, store and factory. The world cries out for such: he is needed and needed badly – the man who can 'Carry a Message to Garcia.'" –Elbert Hubbard

Hubbard says, "The world will make a place for the man (or woman) who can deliver a message to Garcia." Here's hoping that you are one of the few men or women that can deliver the message.

STRENGTH

12.5

LEGACY
LEADERSHIP

The strength to consistently execute leadership at legacy level, in order to achieve your deserved legacy.

Got Legacy?

Everyone leaves a legacy. The only question is *what kind?*

Pieces of your legacy are created with your every action, your every achievement, and your every victory – every day. Legacy also includes failures and recoveries. That's why *resilience* is such an important factor in your leadership mastery.

Legacy matters not just to you, but also to all who love you, and all who you love.

Legacy matters to all who seek to follow you, or your philosophy, or your teachings, or the examples that you have set during your life. And maybe even some who seek to follow in your footsteps.

At some point in your life, legacy will become important to you. Mine became important March the 22nd of 1992. That's the day my first column appeared in the *Charlotte Business Journal.* At once I realized that if I could just write 100 more columns, I would have a book. That was the beginning of my legacy thinking.

Columns lead to books. Books lead to legacy.

And so in November of 1994, when *The Sales Bible* was published I realized I was on my way, but I had no idea of what was to follow.

Instinctively I knew that if I just kept writing – more good things would happen. That was 10 books ago. That was three million copies sold ago. That was 500 times on bestseller lists ago. That was 2,000 speeches ago.

Each of those accomplishments (or achievements) was made possible because I dedicated myself to writing. The same way you can begin to dedicate your actions to something that will lead to a greater good. A legacy.

I now have a body of work. Or I should say I am in the middle of creating my body of work. I've published more than one million words – either in books or in articles. And each time something new is published, another milestone is passed, another notch in my legacy belt is created.

FAIR WARNING: Legacy is not without bumps in the road. (Two throat surgeries, family deaths, and other matters of personal and business life.) Legacy is not without struggle. Legacy is certainly not without daily challenge. Life happens as you create your legacy.

You don't develop a legacy in a day. You create your own legacy day by day.

Some Legacies are Obvious.

If I say the names Vince Lombardi, Glenn Warner, Abraham Lincoln, Napoleon Hill, Dale Carnegie, or John Wooden, what thoughts come to your mind? Whatever you're thinking, understand that those people are all major legacy leavers. Those people have all made a positive impact in the lives of others by setting examples, and creating some form of global awareness and acceptance.

Vince Lombardi was tough as nails as a coach and a leader. He was also an encourager and a winner. (NOTE: Lombardi only lost one championship game in his career – Philadelphia Eagles 1960 – I was there, cheering for the Eagles!)

John Wooden's record and legacy will never be matched. Nine NCAA championships, and an exemplary life of leadership values that he recorded, and lived every day.

Abraham Lincoln was nicknamed "Honest Abe." It was part if his lore, his spoken word, his philosophy, and certainly his legacy. How would that nickname apply to the legacy of today's most celebrated people? Regardless of their accomplishments, would they give that nickname to Bill Clinton? Honest Bill? Honest Barry (Bonds)? Honest Roger (Clemens)? Honest Pete (Rose)? Honest Tiger (Woods)? Hardly. What's your nickname?

Napoleon Hill and Dale Carnegie are the founding fathers of today's personal development and positive attitude. They are authors who wrote their books more than 70 years ago, and still sell hundreds of thousands of copies annually.

Some are unknown by name, until you know their story. Glenn Warner was a tough left guard and captain on the football team of Cornell University in the early 1890s.

He became the head coach at the University of Georgia in 1895 for the salary of $34.00 a week, and went undefeated in his second year. He went on to coach at Cornell, then the Carlisle Indian Industrial School, where he coached the legendary Jim Thorpe.

Then the University of Pittsburgh where he won 33 straight games and three national championships, only losing 12 games in nine years! He coached four other teams in his career and added another national championship at Stanford.

He wrote a book on coaching in 1912 (I own a first edition). In it, he explained his ground-breaking innovations to the game of football. Warner brought many creative playing mechanics to college football:

- **the screen pass**
- **the spiral punt**
- **single-wing and double-wing formations**
- **the use of shoulder and thigh pads**
- **a redesigned helmet for more head safety**

In March 1934, the now legendary collegiate football coach (Carlisle, Pittsburgh, Stanford) Glenn Warner came to Philadelphia to coach Temple University's Owls.

One month later, on a stormy spring night, he was the only one from among seven invited college coaches to show up to give a speech at a youth football banquet and business meeting that Frank Polumbo (noted mobster), and Joe Tomlin (noted mob lawyer) had arranged.

FYI, Glenn Warner had a middle name: "Pop."

At the close of the evening, the Junior Football League of Philadelphia was renamed the "Pop Warner Conference."

Thanks to the Pop Warner name, the Conference grew to 144 teams by 1936 and the city fathers began to credit Pop Warner Football with helping to combat juvenile delinquency. In 1947 the first Pop Warner Santa Claus Bowl was held.

Today, the Pop Warner Little Scholars (also known as Pop Warner, Pop Warner Football, and Junior Football Conference) is still a non-profit organization that provides youth American football, cheerleading, and dance programs for participants in 43 U.S. states and several countries around the world. Consisting of more than 400,000 young people each year, ranging from ages 5 to 16 years old, Pop Warner is the largest and oldest national youth football, cheer, and dance organization in the United States. It is also the only youth sports organization with an academic requirement.

THAT IS LEGACY.

Every one of those "legacy" people, and thousands more just like them, worked hard until the last minute of their last day. *Be one of those people.*

Leave one of those legacies.

Want a great legacy?

- **Be a great person**

- **Live your philosophy**

- **Be happy on the inside**

- **Consistently perform at your highest level**

- **Give more than you take**

KEY ACTION TO TAKE: I recommend you begin reading stories and biographies about leaders who have created and left their legacies. Military leaders, business leaders, coaches, and even politicians. Learn their stories and the actions they took to create legacy. Their stories will inspire yours.

Leadership Affirmations

The following affirmations should be read at least once a month. Post them on a wall in plain sight. Use them as desktop wallpaper on your computer. And record them in your own voice to playback often on your iPod or MP3 player.

I am a leader.

I'm not afraid to decide. When anything goes wrong, I face reality, and decide what's best for everyone, not just myself.

I know how to respond in an instant. Just do what's best. Just do the right thing.

I'm candid in the moment.

I think on my feet, and when someone knocks me on my ass.

I'm not afraid to talk without a script.

I'm not afraid to make a mistake.

I take responsibility for my decisions and my errors – I take "blame" out of the leadership equation.

I tell the truth, so I don't have to mince my words, or have to remember what I said.

I earn respect.

I earn trust.

I select the best people to help me lead (not my best friends) – I will attract the best people in the country, and the best people in the world.

When people offer their help, I will accept their offers as often as I can.

I set goals with my people, not for them.

I stand up for what is right.

I won't back down from those who seek to harm us.

I won't back down from those who oppose freedom.

I speak from strength and conviction.

I listen with the intent to understand.

I don't ask for respect, I earn it.

People may not like my decisions, but they will like me personally.

I am resilient.

I recover quickly and with a resilient attitude.

I resolve to do better next time.

I do everything I can to build and maintain my reputation.

I'm not just a leader. I'm a student of leadership.

The Golden Rule of Leadership, and Life.

I don't believe The Golden Rule applies to leadership.

The real world of snap decisions, safety, success, emergencies, competition, and events on the edges of reality may create a leadership mindset that precludes "Golden Rule thinking."

You can't always employ the do unto others process. In fact, it's probably not even in your mind as you process decisions, and delegate tasks.

There's a simpler rule of leadership that will help you achieve more, cause less doubt among your people, and actually ensure long-term success – even legacy.

DO THE RIGHT THING ALL THE TIME.

Simple, meaningful, effective, and powerful.

Jeffrey Gitomer
Chief Executive Salesman

AUTHOR. Jeffrey is the author of *The New York Times* best sellers *The Sales Bible*, *The Little Red Book of Selling*, *The Little Black Book of Connections*, and *The Little Gold Book of YES! Attitude*. All of his books have been number one best sellers on Amazon.com. Jeffrey's books have sold millions of copies worldwide.

IN FRONT OF MILLIONS OF READERS EVERY WEEK. Jeffrey's syndicated column *Sales Moves* appears in scores of business journals and newspapers in the United States and Europe, and is read by more than four million people every week.

SALES CAFFEINE. Jeffrey's weekly e-zine, *Sales Caffeine*, is a sales wake-up call delivered every Tuesday morning to more than 500,000 subscribers worldwide, free of charge. *Sales Caffeine* allows Jeffrey to communicate valuable sales information, strategies, and answers to sales professionals on a timely basis. To sign up, or for more information, visit www.salescaffeine.com.

MORE THAN 100 PRESENTATIONS A YEAR. Jeffrey gives public and corporate seminars, runs annual sales meetings, and conducts live and Internet training programs on selling, customer loyalty, and personal development.

AWARD FOR PRESENTATION EXCELLENCE. In 1997, Jeffrey was awarded the designation of Certified Speaking Professional (CSP) by the National Speakers Association. The CSP award has been given fewer than 500 times in the past 25 years and is the association's highest earned award.

SPEAKER HALL OF FAME. In 2008, Jeffrey was elected by his peers to the National Speaker Association's Speaker Hall of Fame. The designation, CPAE (Counsel of Peers Award for Excellence), honors professional speakers who have reached the top echelon of performance excellence.

ON THE INTERNET. Jeffrey's WOW! websites get more than 100,000 hits per week from readers and seminar attendees. His state-of-the-art presence on the web and e-commerce ability has set the standard among peers, and has won huge praise and acceptance from customers.

TRAINONE ONLINE SALES TRAINING. Award-winning online sales training lessons are available at www.trainone.com. The content is pure Jeffrey – fun, pragmatic, real world – and can be immediately implemented. TrainOne's innovation is leading the way in the field of customized e-learning.

SALES ASSESSMENT ONLINE. The world's first customized sales assessment, renamed a "successment," will judge your selling skill level in 12 critical areas of sales knowledge and give you a diagnostic report that includes 50 mini sales lessons. This amazing tool will help you rate your sales abilities and explain your opportunities for sales growth. This program is aptly named KnowSuccess because you can't know success until you know yourself.

ACE OF SALES. The first program that actually helps you make sales! Wanna make more sales, close more deals, AND build loyal relationships? Ace of Sales is the golden ticket of selling and gives you and your people the tools and training to attract, engage, differentiate, thank, stay in touch, and WOW customers. To sign up, visit www.aceofsales.com.

RESILIENT LEADER TRAINING. Buy Gitomer and TrainOne have partnered with The Center for Leadership Studies and are now offering a course in *Resilient Leadership*. This dynamic program will test your strengths, expose your vulnerabilities, and reinforce your resilience as a leader and as a person. For more information, call 704/333-1112.

BIG CORPORATE CUSTOMERS. Jeffrey's customers include Coca-Cola, GE, Oracle, US Foodservice, Caterpillar, BMW, Verizon Wireless, CHUBB, MacGregor Golf, Ferguson Enterprises, Kimpton Hotels, Hilton, Enterprise Rent-A-Car, AmeriPride, NCR, Thomson Reuters, Comcast Cable, Raymond James, Liberty Mutual Insurance, Principal Financial Group, Wells Fargo Bank, Monsanto, BlueCross BlueShield, Carlsberg, Wausau Insurance, Northwestern Mutual, MetLife, Sports Authority, GlaxoSmithKline, AC Neilsen, IBM, *The New York Post*, and hundreds of others.

Other titles by Jeffrey Gitomer

THE LITTLE TEAL BOOK OF TRUST
(FT Press, 2008)

THE SALES BIBLE, NEW EDITION
(HarperCollins, 2008)

THE LITTLE PLATINUM BOOK OF CHA-CHING!
(FT Press, 2007)

THE LITTLE GREEN BOOK OF GETTING YOUR WAY
(FT Press, 2007)

THE LITTLE GOLD BOOK OF YES! ATTITUDE
(FT Press, 2007)

THE LITTLE BLACK BOOK OF CONNECTIONS
(Bard Press, 2006)

THE LITTLE RED BOOK OF SALES ANSWERS
(FT Press, 2006)

THE LITTLE RED BOOK OF SELLING
(Bard Press, 2004)

CUSTOMER SATISFACTION IS WORTHLESS, CUSTOMER LOYALTY IS PRICELESS
(Bard Press, 1998)